Contents

Introduction

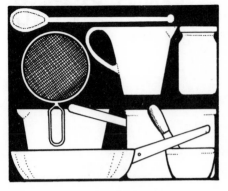

In these days of highly priced vegetables and fruits it is only common sense either to grow your own and then preserve them in various ways for future use or to buy in when there is an abundant supply or glut of the particular items you want and preserve them. Picking your own from large growers is also becoming more popular and brings the price down really low for of course, it cuts out all the overheads otherwise incurred.

Freezing is one excellent way of preserving fruit and vegetables but not everyone owns a deep freeze; so this book concentrates on preserving the produce in other ways. Pickles, chutneys, jams, jellies, and bottling can use up an enormous amount of produce and will keep it in excellent condition if the few simple rules for each particular method of preserving are followed. Commercial chutneys and pickles as well as jams are now very expensive, whilst home processing is neither difficult nor very costly and the results are often so much better than the commercial equivalent. Also there is such enormous scope for mixing and altering ingredients and flavours in favourite preserves to create exciting new and even better ones.

Only use fresh crisp vegetables for pickling. Damaged or blemished produce will not keep well or give good results when finished so is better used in chutneys when the marked part can be cut out and discarded. Windfall apples can, however, be used if the correct weight is made up after cutting out the damaged part of the fruit.

Vegetables need to be brined before pickling to remove the surplus water. If this is omitted the water in the vegetables will dilute the vinegar so that it will not be strong enough to preserve the vegetables and they will go off. Use table salt to make the brine allowing 50g (2oz) per 600ml (1pt) water; and rinse the vegetables in cold running water after removing from the brine or the resulting pickle will be too salty.

Equipment for Pickles and Chutneys

To prevent an unpleasant metallic taste forming in the finished pickle or chutney, all pans made of brass, copper and iron must be avoided. Instead use enamel-lined pans or those made of aluminium or stainless steel. This includes basins and bowls used for brining so always use glass or china for this stage. For the same reason do not use metal sieves but always have a nylon or hair one at hand. Keep one or two large wooden spoons especially for pickle- and chutney-making for the flavour does become attached and might be passed on to something else the spoon is used for.

Jars used for pickling, as for all

preserves, must be sound and clean. They can be ordinary jam jars or special pickling (or bottling) jars but they must be properly covered with a special vinegar-proof top to prevent the evaporation of vinegar during storage which causes the preserve to shrink badly and the surface to dry out into a tough leathery skin, which ruins the pickle or chutney. So use one of the following covers :

1   Special preserving skin sold in rolls to be cut off to the required size, or a vinegar-proof paper.

2   Metal or Bakelite caps which have a special vinegar-proof lining (without the lining the acid in the preserve will eat through the metal).

3   Large corks which are first boiled for 10 minutes in water before use and then covered with greaseproof paper and tied down firmly with string.

4   Greaseproof paper covers which are then covered with a circle of muslin which has been dipped in melted paraffin wax or fat, tied down with string, which then sets firm when it dries out.

All jars should be well filled and covered with a waxed disc (except with pickles with pieces of vegetable or fruit in vinegar or a syrup), keeping the waxed side touching the preserve. Chutneys, jams and jellies are usually covered with a vinegar-proof top or dampened cellophane cover whilst still hot, but marmalades are more usually covered when cold. Jars must be wiped down and clearly labelled with name of preserve and the date. All pickles and chutneys need a little time to mature before use but the times recommended vary and are stated in the individual recipes.

Vinegar

The vinegar used in pickles and preserves is the preserving agent and is obviously very important. Because of this it is advisable to use the best quality vinegar whether it be malt or distilled (white). The colour is no indication of strength but the malt vinegar often gives a better flavour to chutneys. However, the white vinegar (turned colourless only by further distilling) gives a much better appearance to light coloured pickles such as onions, cucumber, cauliflower, etc, but has the same preserving qualities as malt vinegar. To give the spicy flavour to the pickles, the vinegar is usually infused with spices and herbs which flavour the vegetables, etc. Commercial spiced vinegar is now available in small bottles and bulk containers but recipes for spicing vinegar are given in the book.

Note Remember chutneys are cooked in an uncovered pan to allow the necessary evaporation. If something is cooked in a covered pan the recipe will say so, otherwise in this book leave the lid off the pan. One metric teaspoon : 5ml ; one metric tablespoon : 15ml.

3

Pickles

Pickled Cucumber

Ingredients

3 cucumbers
450g (1lb) onions
45ml (3 level tbsp) salt
600ml (1pt) white vinegar
175g (6oz) caster sugar
7.5ml (1½ level tsp) celery seed
5ml (1 level tsp) mustard seed

Wipe the cucumbers and slice thinly. Put into a large bowl. Peel the onions and slice thinly and then mix with the cucumbers. Sprinkle with the salt, mix well and leave to stand for about an hour. Pour off the brine, rinse the cucumber and onion thoroughly in cold water and then drain very well. Put the vinegar into a saucepan with the sugar, celery seed and mustard seed and heat gently until the sugar has dissolved. Bring to the boil and boil for 3 minutes. Pack the cucumber and onion slices tightly into jars and cover completely with the hot vinegar. Cover at once whilst hot with a vinegar-proof top and store in a cool dry place for 2–3 weeks before use.

Pickled Mushrooms

Ingredients

900g (2lb) small young mushrooms
White vinegar
3–4 blades of mace
5ml (1 level tsp) white pepper
10ml (2 level tsp) salt
7.5ml (1½ level tsp) ground ginger
1 onion, peeled and finely chopped
  (optional)
1 bayleaf (optional)

If using cultivated mushrooms just trim off the stalks. With field mushrooms, unless they are the tight button ones, trim off the stalks and peel carefully. Wash all mushrooms thoroughly in salted water and drain well. Discard any damaged or blemished ones. Either put mushrooms into a saucepan or an ovenproof casserole adding just sufficient vinegar to cover and then mix in all the other ingredients. Bring slowly up to the boil on the top of the cooker and simmer very gently until just tender and the mushrooms have shrunk ; or cover casserole and cook in a cool oven 170°C (325°F) mark 3 for about 20 minutes or until tender. Remove the mushrooms and pack into clean jars. Strain the vinegar and bring back to the boil. Pour the hot liquid over the mushrooms to cover completely. Cover at once whilst hot with a vinegar-proof top.

Note 350g (¾lb) raw mushrooms will usually fill a 450g (1lb) jar but it will vary with the larger and smaller mushrooms.

Apple and Onion Pickle

Ingredients

900g (2lb) cooking apples (or windfalls)
900g (2lb) onions
100g (4oz) sultanas
2.5ml (½ level tsp) whole peppercorns
20 cloves
50g (2oz) chillies
2 pieces root ginger, bruised
30ml (2 level tbsp) salt
1.1l (2pt) white or malt vinegar
50g (2oz) demerara sugar (optional)

Peel, core and chop the apples and plunge them immediately into boiling water for 3 minutes. Drain very thoroughly. This will prevent apples from discolouring and tenderize them sufficiently for the pickle. Peel the onions and chop finely ; then mix with the apples and sultanas. Pack into hot dry jars. Tie the peppercorns, cloves, chillies and ginger in a piece of muslin and place in a saucepan with the salt, vinegar and sugar, if used. Leave to infuse for 1 hour then bring up to the boil and simmer for 10 minutes. Remove the muslin bag and pour the boiling vinegar into the jars to completely cover the contents. Cover with vinegar-proof tops whilst still hot and store in a cool, dry place for 1–2 weeks before using.

Preparing Spiced Vinegar

There is a quick and a slow method of making a spiced vinegar and although the quick method is more often used, the longer soaking of the slow method gives better results. With both ordinary spiced and sweet spiced vinegar use one of these methods :
Either put the vinegar with all the spices into a saucepan and bring slowly to the boil. Pour into a bowl, cover with a plate and leave to stand for at least 2 hours or until cold. Strain and use as required. Or put the cold vinegar into a large container with all the spices and cover tightly with a vinegar-proof top. Leave to stand for about 2 months before straining off to use. Both vinegars will keep for some time after spicing.

Recipes for spiced vinegar are given in the book.

Pickles

Pickled Onions

Ingredients

2.7–4.5kg (6–10lb) pickling onions
900g (2lb) salt
Water

Spiced Vinegar

2l (3½pt) vinegar, white or malt
15g (½oz) blade mace
15g (½oz) whole allspice
15g (½oz) whole cloves
Piece of cinnamon stick
12 whole peppercorns

Choose small even-sized pickling onions which should be firm and without any sign of sprouting at the top. Wash, then place in a large container. Make a brine of 4.5l (1gal) water to 450g (1lb) salt, pour over the onions and leave to soak for 12 hours. Drain onions, peel and replace in a fresh brine made in the same way and leave to soak for 24–36 hours. Make the spiced vinegar by putting all the ingredients into a pan and bringing slowly up to the boil. Pour into a bowl, cover and leave until cold—at least 3 hours. Strain and use. (If individual spices are unavailable use 50–75g [2–3oz] pickling spice but this will probably give a little different flavour each time, for commercially packed pickling spice differs from make to make and availability of spices. There is also a commercial spiced vinegar available on the market packed in 1.1l [2pt] and 4.5l [1 gal] containers.)

Remove the onions from the brine, and drain very well. Pack into jars or bottles as tightly as possible and cover with cold spiced vinegar. Cover with a vinegar-proof top and label the jars. Store in a cool dry place for 3 months before using.

Pickled Cauliflower

Ingredients

2–3 medium sized cauliflowers
100g (4oz) salt
1.1l (2pt) vinegar—white or malt
4 blades of mace
15ml (1tbsp) whole allspice
15ml (1tbsp) whole cloves
Piece cinnamon stick
6 whole peppercorns

Use firm tight headed cauliflowers and break into small florets, discarding the tough stalks and leaves. Make a brine with the salt and 1.1l (2pt) water and put in the cauliflower. Cover and leave to soak overnight. The next day rinse off surplus salt from the cauliflower and drain thoroughly. Pack tightly into jars. Put the vinegar into a saucepan with the spices and bring slowly up to

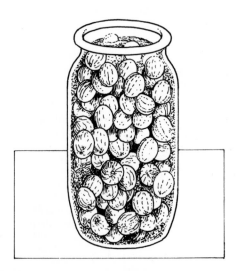

the boil. Pour into a bowl, cover and leave to stand for at least 2 hours. Strain the cold vinegar and pour into the jars to cover the cauliflower. Cover with a vinegar-proof top and store in a cool, dry place for 6–8 weeks before use.

Pickled Red Cabbage

Ingredients

1 large firm red cabbage (about 2kg [5lb])
Salt

Spiced Vinegar

1.1l (2pt) vinegar
6–8 blades of mace
15ml (1tbsp) whole allspice
15ml (1tbsp) whole cloves
Piece of cinnamon stick
6 whole peppercorns

Remove any limp, marked and tatty outside leaves from the cabbage then cut it into quarters. Remove the hard white core from the centre of the cabbage and then slice each quarter into fine shreds. This can be done either by using a sharp knife or by using a hand shredding machine or an electric shredder. Place the shredded cabbage in a large bowl layering it up with salt. Cover bowl and leave to stand overnight. To make the spiced vinegar put all the ingredients into a pan and bring slowly up to the boil. Pour into a bowl, cover and leave until cold —at least 3 hours. Strain and use. (If individual spices are unavailable use 40g [1½oz] pickling spice from a packet.) The next day drain the cabbage, rinse off the salt and drain again very thoroughly. Pack fairly tightly into jars and cover completely with cold spiced vinegar. Cover with a vinegar-proof top. Store for about a week before using in a cool dry place.

Note Pickled cabbage should be used fairly quickly for it tends to go limp after 2–3 months.

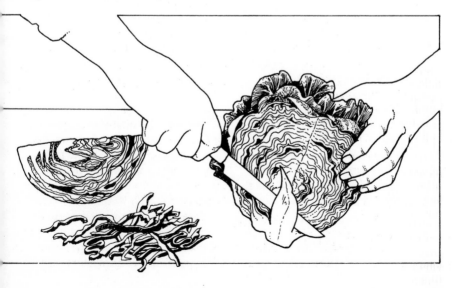

Pickles

Pickled Gherkins

Ingredients

450g (1lb) gherkins
Salt
600ml (1pt) vinegar—white or malt
5ml (1 level tsp) black peppercorns
5ml (1 level tsp) whole allspice
3–4 cloves
1 blade of mace

Wash the gherkins, do not peel ; trim and place in a bowl. Make up a brine using 100g (4oz) salt to 1.1l (2pt) water and pour over the gherkins. Cover and leave to soak for 3 days. Drain gherkins, rinse off the salt and drain again and then pack into large jars. Put the vinegar into a saucepan with the spices, bring to the boil and simmer for 10 minutes. Pour the hot vinegar over the gherkins, cover tightly and leave in a warm place for about 24 hours. Strain off the vinegar, boil it up and pour back over the gherkins. Cover and leave for another 24 hours. Repeat this process several times until the gherkins become a good green colour. Strain off the vinegar again. Pack the gherkins evenly and tightly into fairly small jars and cover with the boiling vinegar. Seal at once with a vinegar-proof top and leave for several weeks before use. (Extra spiced vinegar may be required for the final topping up in which case make half the above quantity.)

Note Gherkins are the fruit of a small variety of cucumber, but are not always easy to get hold of. The best varieties to use are small and dark green with a rough skin, but small ridge or immature cucumbers can also be used if they are not longer than 6–7.5cm (2½–3in). For sweet pickled gherkins add 50–75g (2–3oz) demerara sugar for malt vinegar or white sugar for white vinegar per 600ml (1pt).

Pickled Beetroot

Ingredients

1.4–1.8kg (3–4lb) young beetroots
Salt
About 1.3l (2¼pt) spiced vinegar (see pickled cabbage)

Wash the beetroots thoroughly taking care not to damage the skins. Put into a saucepan and cover with water adding 25g (1oz) salt per 600ml (1pt). Bring to the boil, cover and simmer gently until tender, about 1½–2 hours depending on size. (Beetroots can also be wrapped in foil and baked in a moderate oven 180°C (350°F) mark 4 for 1¼–2 hours or until tender.) Cool beetroots then carefully rub off the skins and remove any blemishes from the flesh. Cut into thin slices or dice the beetroots. Pack into jars and cover with cold spiced vinegar adding 15g (½oz) salt per 600ml (1pt) if the beetroots were baked in foil. Cover with a vinegar-proof top. Store in a cool dry place for at least two weeks before using and use up within 3–4 months for the beetroot to stay in prime condition.

Note For longer storage pack diced beetroot fairly loosely into 450g (1lb) jars and cover with boiling spiced vinegar. Cover as above and keep for

at least a month before using.
The delicious tiny beetroots about
the size of a walnut can be pickled
whole.

Red Tomato Pickle

Ingredients

1.4kg (3lb) red tomatoes
75g (3oz) salt
450g (1lb) brown sugar
600ml (1pt) vinegar—brown or white
1–2 cloves garlic, crushed
1 blade of mace
Piece of cinnamon stick
5ml (1 level tsp) whole allspice

Peel tomatoes, if liked, by plunging
first into boiling water for about 20
seconds and then into cold water, or
wipe over carefully. Cut into thick
slices. Make up a strong brine using
75g (3oz) salt to 600ml (1pt) water
and add the tomatoes ; leave to soak
for 4–5 hours. Rinse off excess salt and
drain well. Put the sugar, vinegar, garlic,
mace and allspice in a saucepan and
heat gently until the sugar dissolves
then bring to the boil. Add the
tomatoes, bring back to the boil and
simmer for 2 minutes. Carefully remove
the tomatoes and pack straight away in
layers into hot clean jars. Boil the
vinegar until it begins to thicken, then
strain and pour over the tomatoes to
fill the jars. Cover at once with a
vinegar-proof top, and label. Store in
a cool dry place for 1–2 weeks before
using.

Note When available yellow tomatoes
can also be pickled in this way. Tiny
tomatoes (red or yellow) can be peeled
and left whole to pickle.

Pickles

Mixed Pickle

Ingredients

1kg (2½lb) prepared mixed vegetables
(eg cauliflower, small cucumbers,
shallots, French beans, etc.)
Salt

Spiced Vinegar

1.1l (2pt) vinegar
3–4 blades of mace
15ml (1tbsp) whole allspice
15ml (1tbsp) whole cloves
Piece of cinnamon stick
6 whole peppercorns

Cut the cauliflower into small florets
discarding tough stalks and leaves ;
peel and dice the cucumber (or wipe
and leave the skin on if preferred) ;
peel the shallots ; top and tail and cut
beans into 1–2cm (½–¾in) slices. Put
all the vegetables into a bowl sprinkling
liberally with salt, cover and leave for
48 hours in a cool place ; or if
preferred make a brine using 100g
(4oz) salt to 2 pints water, add the
vegetables and leave to soak for
24 hours. Make the spiced vinegar by
putting all the ingredients into a
saucepan and bring slowly up to the
boil. Pour into a bowl, cover and leave
until cold—at least 3 hours. Strain and
use. (If individual spices are
unavailable use 40–50g [1½–2oz]
pickling spice.) Wash off all the salt
from the vegetables and drain very
thoroughly. Pack the vegetables neatly
into jars but not too tightly or the
vinegar will not have room to circulate
freely. Fill up with cold spiced vinegar,
cover with vinegar-proof tops and
label. Store in a cool dry place for at
least 2 weeks before using.

Piccalilli

This is a special type of pickle which is
a great favourite with many people
because of its spicy mustard sauce.
It is delicious with all cold meats and
is useful for sandwiches and to serve
with snacks.

10

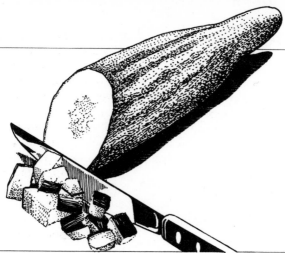

Ingredients

2.7kg (6lb) prepared vegetables
(eg cucumber, beans, small onions,
marrow, cauliflower, green tomatoes,
etc)
450g (1lb) salt
250g (9oz) caster sugar
20g ($\frac{3}{4}$oz) dry mustard
10ml (2 level tsp) ground ginger
1.7l (3pt) white vinegar
60ml (4 level tbsp) flour or cornflour
25–30ml (1$\frac{1}{2}$–2 level tbsp) turmeric

Either peel or wipe the cucumber then
cut into dice ; top, tail and slice the
beans ; peel onions and cut in half or
quarters if large ; peel, remove seeds
and dice the marrow ; cut cauliflower
into small florets discarding tough
stalks and leaves ; cut green tomatoes
into small pieces, if used. Either layer up
the prepared vegetables with the salt
in a large bowl or make a brine by
adding it to 4.5l (1gal) water, and add
the vegetables ; leave for 24 hours
keeping the vegetables under the brine
with a weighted plate. Drain the
vegetables and rinse off all the salt and
then drain again very thoroughly. Mix
the sugar, mustard and ginger with
1.5l (2$\frac{1}{2}$pt) of the vinegar in a large
saucepan then add all the drained
vegetables. Bring slowly up to the boil
and simmer gently for 10–20 minutes
until the vegetables are tender-crisp
(or tender, if preferred) but not soft and
mushy. Blend the flour and turmeric
into the remaining vinegar until
smooth and stir into the cooked
vegetables. Bring back to the boil for
2–3 minutes. Pack the vegetables into
hot clean jars as tightly as possible,
filling up with more sauce. Cover
whilst still hot with vinegar-proof tops,
and label. Store in a cool dry place for
at least 2 weeks before using.

Note For a hot sharp piccalilli (instead
of the sweeter milder recipe given
above) use the same vegetables and
salt as above but use the following
ingredients for the sauce, making it in
the same way : 15g ($\frac{1}{2}$oz) turmeric ;
40g (1$\frac{1}{2}$oz) dry mustard ; 25–40g
(1–1$\frac{1}{2}$oz) ground ginger ; 20g ($\frac{3}{4}$oz)
flour or cornflour ; 175g (6oz) white
sugar and 1.1l (2pt) white vinegar.

Sweet Pickles

This sweet type of pickle is often preferred to the more vinegary types and it is a particularly good accompaniment to cold meats. As well as having a higher proportion of sugar added to the vinegar, they are usually made with all fruit or at least more fruit than vegetable. Whole fruits to be pickled need pricking with a darning needle, cocktail stick or thin skewer before heating otherwise they will shrivel up during pickling. A brine is not usually necessary for this type of pickle for the excess moisture evaporates during cooking, unlike the vegetables which have little or no cooking.

Pickled Pears

Ingredients

900g (2lb) hard pears
900g (2lb) white sugar
900ml (1½pt) white vinegar
Few whole cloves

Peel the pears, quarter and remove the cores, then cut the flesh into dice. Cook the pears in a little boiling water until just soft then drain very well. Meanwhile put the sugar, water and cloves into a saucepan, heat gently until the sugar dissolves, then bring to the boil and simmer for about 20 minutes. Add the well drained fruit to the syrup and continue to boil for a further 15 minutes. Pour into hot jars, filling well with the pears and cover at once with vinegar-proof tops. Store in a cool dry place for 6 months before using.

Spiced Pears

Ingredients

2.7kg (6lb) hard pears (small or medium sized)
400g (14oz) white sugar
15–20ml (3–4 level tsp) salt
1.1l (2pt) water
1.1l (2pt) distilled or white wine vinegar
2 cinnamon sticks
Strip of thinly pared lemon rind
5ml (1 level tsp) whole cloves

Peel the pears, cut into quarters and remove the cores. Dissolve 50g (2oz) sugar and the salt in the water and bring slowly to the boil making sure the sugar is dissolved. Add the pears to the boiling water, remove from the heat and cover tightly. Leave to stand until cool. Put the remaining sugar into a pan with the vinegar, cinnamon sticks, lemon rind and cloves and heat gently until the sugar dissolves; then bring to the boil. Drain the pears very well and add to the vinegar syrup in the pan. Bring back to the boil then remove from the heat and leave to get cold. Boil up again slowly and repeat the cooling and boiling process twice more. Leave to get cold once more then pack the pears into small jars and cover with the syrup. Do not seal jars but fill up for the next four days with the surplus syrup until no more syrup is absorbed by the fruit; then cover as usual with a vinegar-proof top. Keep for several weeks before using.

Note Spiced pears are excellent with pork.

Pickled Peaches

Ingredients

900g (2lb) white sugar
600ml (1pt) white vinegar
15g ($\frac{1}{2}$oz) whole cloves
15ml ($\frac{1}{2}$oz) whole allspice
Small piece of cinnamon stick
Small piece of root ginger, bruised
Thinly pared rind of 1 lemon or orange
1.8kg (4lb) freestone peaches

Dissolve the sugar slowly in the vinegar. Crush the spices and tie in a piece of muslin with the cinnamon stick, ginger and lemon or orange rind

and add to the saucepan. Cut the peaches into quarters then remove the stones and carefully remove the peel. (If peaches are difficult to peel, dip the whole fruit quickly first into boiling water and then into cold water and then the skins should easily rub off. Cut into quarters and remove the stones after peeling.) Add the quartered peaches to the syrup and simmer gently until the peaches are just soft. Drain the fruit and pack neatly and fairly tightly into small warm jars. Boil the syrup hard until it begins to thicken. Pour sufficient syrup over the fruit to cover and fill up the jars. Cover with a vinegar-proof top whilst still hot. Store for 2–3 months before using.

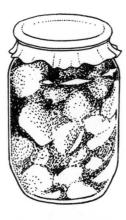

Note In freestone fruit the skin and stone separate easily whereas with cling-stone varieties the flesh is firmer and is firmly attached to the stone thus making it difficult to cut the fruit into neat quarters or slices.

Sweet Pickles

Pickled Plums

Ingredients

1.4kg (3lb) Victoria plums
300ml ($\frac{1}{2}$pt) white vinegar
450g (1lb) white sugar
25g (1oz) ground cinnamon
5ml (1 level tsp) mixed spice

Remove stalks from the plums, wipe them over well and discard any which are bruised or have bad blemishes. Prick each plum two or three times with a wooden cocktail stick or small skewer to prevent them from shrivelling up during the pickling process. Place the fruit in a deep bowl. Put the vinegar into a saucepan with the sugar and spices and heat gently until the sugar dissolves, then bring up to the boil and boil until slightly reduced. Strain through a double layer of muslin and then bring back to the boil in a clean saucepan. Pour over the

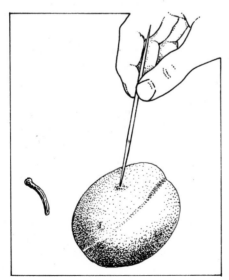

plums, cover bowl and leave for 2 days. Strain off the syrup and bring back to the boil. Pour over the plums again and leave for 2–3 days. Strain off the syrup again and boil up in a pan. Pack the plums into small jars and cover with warm syrup. Cover at once with a vinegar-proof top. Store for 6–8 weeks before using.

Note Other varieties of plums may be used.

Pickled Damsons

Ingredients

1.8kg (4lb) firm ripe damsons
900g (2lb) white sugar
600ml (1pt) white vinegar
1 blade mace
Small piece root ginger
5ml (1 level tsp) ground allspice
10ml (2 level tsp) ground cloves
Piece of thinly pared lemon rind

Remove the stems from the fruit, wash well and dry ; then prick each damson twice with a cocktail stick or fine skewer. Put the sugar, vinegar and spices into a saucepan and heat gently until the fruit is almost tender—but take care not to let the skins break. Drain well and pack the fruit into small clean jars. Boil the syrup until slightly reduced —about 10 minutes—then strain through a double layer of muslin and pour into the jars to cover the fruit. The next day strain off the syrup and boil up then pour back over the damsons. Repeat this process for the next 2–3 days. Cover with a vinegar-proof top whilst still hot and label. Store in a cool, dry place for a few weeks before use.

Pickled Rhubarb

Ingredients

1.4kg (3lb) prepared young tender
rhubarb
900g (2lb) white sugar
600ml (1pt) white vinegar
15g ($\frac{1}{2}$oz) whole cloves
7.5ml (1$\frac{1}{2}$ level tsp) whole allspice
15–25g ($\frac{1}{2}$–1oz) whole root ginger,
bruised
Small piece of cinnamon stick
Thinly pared rind of $\frac{1}{2}$ lemon

Wash the rhubarb and dry well then
cut into 2cm ($\frac{3}{4}$in) lengths. Put the
sugar into a saucepan with the vinegar
and spices and heat gently until the
sugar dissolves. Add the rhubarb and
simmer very gently until the fruit is
almost tender—but take great care not
to let it break up and become mushy.
Leave to get cold then strain off all the
syrup, and the spices (optional). Pack
the rhubarb into small warmed jars ;
reboil the syrup until syrupy—about
10 minutes—and then pour into the
jars to cover the fruit. Cover at once
with vinegar-proof tops whilst still hot
and label. Store in a dark, cool and dry
place for 6–8 weeks before use.

Spiced Orange Rings

Ingredients

8–10 firm medium-sized oranges
900ml (1$\frac{1}{2}$pt) white vinegar
675g (1$\frac{1}{2}$lb) white sugar
15ml (1 level tbsp) ground cloves
2 pieces cinnamon stick
5ml (1 level tsp) whole cloves

Wipe the oranges thoroughly,
scrubbing off any stubborn marks, but
do not peel. Cut into thin even slices
0.5cm ($\frac{1}{4}$in) thick. Put the oranges into
a saucepan in layers and barely cover
with water. Bring to the boil, cover and
simmer gently for about $\frac{3}{4}$ hour or until
the orange rind is really tender. Drain
well and put the cooking liquid back
into a saucepan with the vinegar, sugar
and spices. Heat gently until the sugar
dissolves then bring up to the boil and
simmer for 10 minutes. Replace the
orange rings a few at a time in the
syrup and simmer gently until the rind
becomes clear. Remove the rings
straight to warm jars and pack neatly.
Continue with all the orange rings.
Boil the syrup again until it begins to
thicken and then leave to cool but not
get cold. Strain and pour over the
orange rings to cover and fill the jars.
Add a few of the cloves to each jar and
cover with a vinegar-proof top. Store
in a cool, dark place for several weeks
before using.

Note These orange rings are particularly
good served with cold ham, turkey,
chicken and duck and make very
attractive gifts.

Vinegars

Fruit Vinegars

These are usually made with soft fruits and are used like a cordial. Fruit which is in good condition but which is a little bruised or too wet for freezing or jam is excellent for this purpose. Fruit vinegars used to be an old-fashioned remedy for curing sore throats and colds, and can also be used to replace wine vinegar in salad dressings to give unusual flavours and colours to the salads.

The prepared and washed fruits are put into a large glass or china bowl and roughly broken up with a wooden spoon. Add 600ml (1pt) white wine vinegar or best malt vinegar per 450g (1lb) fruit to the bowl and mix lightly. Cover the bowl with a cloth and leave to stand for 3–4 days giving an occasional stir. Then strain off the liquid through a double layer of muslin into a large saucepan. Add 450g (1lb) white sugar to each pint of juice and heat gently until the sugar dissolves. Bring up to the boil and boil for 10 minutes then cool and pour into warmed clean dry bottles. Cork tightly and label. Blackberries, raspberries and blackcurrants are the most usual fruits to use.

Flavoured Vinegars

Home-made herb flavoured vinegars are very useful in the kitchen—it is a simple process but takes time, usually from two to six weeks, for the vinegar to absorb the flavour of the herbs. A wide mouthed jar should be thoroughly cleaned and then half filled with freshly gathered herbs (just before they flower for the best results) eg tarragon, mint, thyme, marjoram or basil. Then fill up the jar with the best vinegar—either malt or white wine. Cover and store in a cool, dry and dark place until sufficiently flavoured. Strain the vinegar through a double layer of muslin, taste and add more vinegar if the herb flavour is too strong (or label the bottle stating that it is double strength). Pour into bottles and cork tightly. Use in salad dressings, mayonnaise, etc.

Preserved Mint in Vinegar

Ingredients

225g ($\frac{1}{2}$lb) freshly picked mint leaves
600ml (1pt) malt vinegar
450g (1lb) white sugar

Wash and dry the mint leaves removing all the stems. Chop the mint finely and put into small wide-necked jars. Put the vinegar into a saucepan with the sugar and heat gently until the sugar dissolves then bring it just up to the boil. Leave to get cold. Pour the vinegar over the mint mixing it lightly until evenly coated then seal the jar to make it airtight. Store in a dark cool place. To use the mint for mint sauce, spoon out a little of the concentrated mint and liquid into a small jug and add sufficient fresh vinegar to give the desired consistency. If it is too strong add a little water in place of the vinegar.

Preserved Horse-radish in Vinegar

Ingredients

Plump horse-radish roots
5ml (1 level tsp) salt
White vinegar

Wash and clean the horse-radish then either scrape, mince or grate it. Plunge immediately into a boiling solution of brine—5ml (1 level tsp) salt to 600ml (1pt) water—for 1 minute. This helps to keep the colour of the horse-radish. Drain thoroughly and pack into small warmed jars. Cover at once with boiling white vinegar and seal to make the jars airtight.

To make the preserved horse-radish into horse-radish cream sauce to serve with roast beef, smoked trout or to use in sandwiches put 15ml (1 level tbsp) into a small bowl and mix in 2.5–5ml ($\frac{1}{2}$–1 level tsp) made mustard, 5ml (1 level tsp) caster sugar, 60ml (4tbsp) double cream, lightly whipped, and salt and pepper to taste.

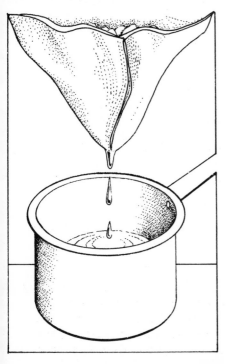
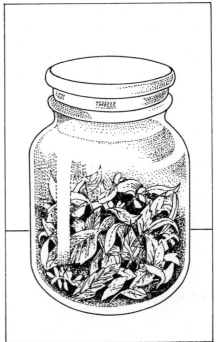

Sauces and Ketchups

Home-made sauces and ketchups usually have one predominating flavour, ie tomato, mushroom, plum, etc with spices added to bring out rather than disguise the main flavour. Remember that sauces and ketchups will thicken more as they cool so take this into consideration during cooking and also remember to use the same types of sieves and pans as for chutneys. In other words use hair, nylon or stainless steel sieves and enamel-lined, stainless steel or aluminium pans, for many metals give an unpleasant metallic taste to chutneys and for this reason avoid using copper, brass or iron pans.

Sauces and ketchups can ferment after bottling so they need to be sterilized immediately after filling as described below:

Ripe Tomato Sauce

Ingredients

10g ($\frac{1}{4}$oz) whole allspice
4–5 blades of mace
Piece of cinnamon stick
600ml (1pt) white vinegar
5.4kg (12lb) ripe tomatoes
40g (1$\frac{1}{2}$oz) salt
Good pinch of cayenne pepper
7.5ml (1$\frac{1}{2}$ level tsp) paprika pepper
30ml (2 tbsp) chilli vinegar
450g (1lb) white sugar

Use bottles with screw tops or corks. Heat the bottles in a cool oven, 150°C (300°F) mark 2 and boil the caps or corks for 10 minutes. Use a deep pan and either put an upturned plate or thick wad of newspaper in the bottom

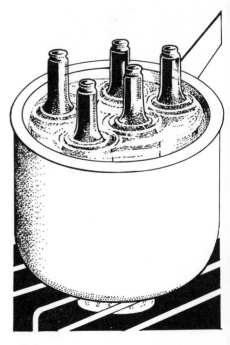

and then stand the filled and sealed jars on this. Fill the pan with cold water to reach the necks of the bottles and then heat gently to reach simmering point 76°C (170°F). Simmer at this heat for 30 minutes. Remove the bottles and stand on a board or pad of cloth and tighten screw-topped bottles or push the corks in further with cork-topped bottles. If using corks, when the bottles are partly cooled they should be coated in melted paraffin wax and secured with wire. Store the cold, labelled bottles in a cool dry place.

Put the spices into a piece of muslin and tie loosely. Put with the vinegar into a pan and bring to the boil. Remove from the heat, cover pan and leave to infuse for 2 hours. Remove spices. Wipe tomatoes and slice. Place in a pan and cook gently without any added liquid until they are pulpy. Rub through a sieve, return to the pan and add the salt, cayenne and paprika and continue to cook gently until the mixture begins to thicken. Then add the spiced vinegar, sugar and chilli vinegar and continue to boil until the mixture thickens to the consistency of thick cream, stirring from time to time. Pour into hot bottles leaving a 2.5cm (1in) headspace and put on screw tops (not too tightly) or corks. Sterilize for 30 minutes, seal tightly, cool and label and store in a cool dry place.

Note If chilli vinegar is unavailable, tarragon or garlic vinegar can be substituted or a little powdered garlic may be added to the sauce and extra vinegar omitted.

Inexpensive Tomato Sauce

Ingredients

900g (2lb) ripe tomatoes, roughly chopped
450g (1lb) cooking apples, peeled, cored and chopped
225g ($\frac{1}{2}$lb) shallots or onions, peeled and chopped
300ml ($\frac{1}{2}$pt) white vinegar
225g ($\frac{1}{2}$lb) white sugar
10ml (2 level tsp) salt
10 whole cloves
3 pieces root ginger, bruised or 10ml (2 level tsp) ground ginger
2–3 chillies

Put the tomatoes, apples and onions in a pan without any extra liquid and cook very gently until soft, in a covered pan. Stir occasionally, and take care not to let the vegetables burn. Add the vinegar, sugar, salt and spices and bring back to the boil. Cover pan and simmer for about $\frac{1}{2}$ hour. Rub the sauce through a sieve and return to a clean pan. Bring back to the boil, and simmer uncovered, for about 15 minutes or until thickened. Pour into hot bottles leaving a 2.5cm (1in) headspace, seal and sterilize for 30 minutes. Complete sealing bottles, cool and label and store in a cool dry place.

Green Tomato Sauce

Ingredients

1.4kg (3lb) green tomatoes, thinly sliced
450g (1lb) cooking apples, peeled, cored and chopped
1 onion or 6–8 shallots, peeled and chopped
225g ($\frac{1}{2}$lb) sugar, brown or white
5ml (1 level tsp) ground pickling spice
2.5ml ($\frac{1}{2}$ level tsp) ground pepper
2.5ml ($\frac{1}{2}$ level tsp) dry mustard
10ml (2 level tsp) salt
2 cloves garlic, crushed (optional)
300ml ($\frac{1}{2}$pt) vinegar—malt or white
Gravy browning to colour (optional)

Put all the ingredients except the gravy browning into a large pan and bring slowly up to the boil, stirring frequently until the sugar has dissolved and everything is well mixed. Cover pan and simmer gently for about an hour, stirring occasionally until very soft. Rub the sauce through a sieve and return to a clean pan. Add gravy browning to give the desired colour and bring the sauce back to the boil. Pour into hot bottles leaving a 2.5cm (1in) headspace and seal and sterilize for 30 minutes. Complete sealing bottles, cool, label and store in a cool, dry place.

Sauces and Ketchups

Plum Sauce

Ingredients

3.6kg (8lb) plums, washed, stoned and
    quartered
450g (1lb) onions, peeled and
    chopped
225g ($\frac{1}{2}$lb) currants, sultanas or
    raisins
1.1l (2pt) vinegar, malt or white
15g ($\frac{1}{2}$oz) root ginger, bruised
15g ($\frac{1}{2}$oz) whole allspice
3–4 chillies
10ml (2tsp) whole peppercorns
5ml (1 level tsp) dry mustard (optional)
Piece of cinnamon stick
450g (1lb) sugar, brown or white
50g (2oz) salt

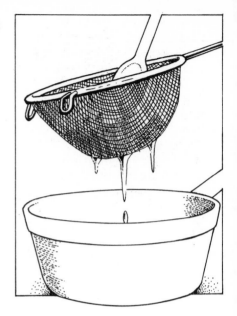

Put the plums into a saucepan with the
onions, currants, 600ml (1pt) vinegar
and all the spices. Bring to the boil,
cover and simmer gently for about
$\frac{1}{2}$ hour or until tender, stirring
occasionally. Rub the sauce through a
sieve and return to a clean pan with
the remaining vinegar, sugar and salt.
Return slowly to the boil, making sure
the sugar has dissolved then simmer
for about 1 hour or until the sauce is
the consistency of thick cream. Pour
into hot bottles leaving a 2.5cm (1in)
headspace and seal and sterilize for
30 minutes. Complete sealing bottles,
cool, label and store in a cool and dry
place.

Note The different coloured plums
which are available will vary the
colour of the finished sauce and malt
vinegar and brown sugar, if used, will
darken the sauce considerably.

Mushroom Ketchup

Ingredients

1.4kg (3lb) mushrooms, washed
75g (3oz) salt
600ml (1pt) vinegar, malt or white
5ml (1 level tsp) whole peppercorns
5ml (1 level tsp) whole allspice
2.5ml ($\frac{1}{2}$ level tsp) ground mace
2.5ml ($\frac{1}{2}$ level tsp) ground ginger
8 whole cloves
Small piece of cinnamon stick

Break the mushrooms up roughly and
place in a bowl. Sprinkle with the salt,
cover and leave to stand for about 12
hours. Rinse off the excess salt and
drain mushrooms well. Place in a
saucepan and mash well with a
wooden spoon. Add the vinegar and
spices and bring to the boil. Cover and
simmer gently for about $\frac{1}{2}$ hour or until
the excess vinegar is absorbed. Press
the liquid out through a fine sieve and

pour quickly into hot bottles leaving a 2.5cm (1in) headspace. Seal and sterilize for 30 minutes then complete the sealing of bottles, cool, label and store in a cool, dry place.

Note Either cultivated or field mushrooms can be used for this recipe but with large field ones it is necessary to remove the stalks and peel them first.

Walnut Ketchup

Ingredients

35–40 green walnuts
75g (3oz) onion or shallots, finely chopped
75g (3oz) salt
900ml (1½pt) spiced vinegar (see pickled onion recipe on p 6)

Use green immature walnuts, before the shells have formed. Test each

walnut by pricking with a needle, and if any shell can be felt, discard the nut. Cut the walnuts in halves and crush them and then place in a bowl with the onions and salt. Bring the vinegar to the boil, pour over the walnuts, stir well to dissolve the salt and leave to stand, in a covered bowl in a cool place, for 5 days. Each day give the mixture a good stir. Pour the liquid through a fine sieve into a saucepan and bring to the boil. Simmer very gently for about 50 minutes then pour into hot bottles. Seal and sterilize for 30 minutes then complete sealing bottles, cool, label and store in a cool, dry place.

Note Commercially prepared spiced vinegar can be used, if preferred.

21

Chutneys

A chutney is a mixture of fruits and/or vegetables, either fresh and/or dried which are cooked with sugar, spices and vinegar until thick and pulpy. The basic ingredients such as apples, plums, red and green tomatoes, pears, gooseberries etc are preserved by the vinegar, spices and salt used in cooking. The additional ingredients such as onions, garlic, dates, sultanas, raisins and spices will add the flavours. Tough vegetables are improved by partly cooking in some of the vinegar before adding the rest of the ingredients. Use brown sugar and brown malt vinegar for richer flavour but white sugar and white distilled vinegar for light coloured produce and to keep its bright colour.

Most chutneys will improve in flavour with keeping and should store for 2–3 years. The finished chutney should be fairly smooth and have a mellow flavour although, once you have achieved a good chutney, the spiciness and sweetness can be altered to your own taste. By mincing part or all of the main ingredients, the texture will be smoother, but chopped ingredients can still give a smooth texture with long slow cooking.

Sieves used for chutneys, as for pickles, must be of hair, nylon or stainless steel, and pans be enamel-lined, stainless steel or aluminium to prevent the unpleasant metallic taste caused by iron, copper and brass. The chutney should be bottled while hot in clean, warmed jars and a vinegar-proof cover used, otherwise, if paper covers are used, the contents will have shrunk badly after a short storage with a very hard and dry top surface. Metal caps can be used if they are well lacquered, fitting plastic covers are suitable and a special vinegar-proof paper is available which

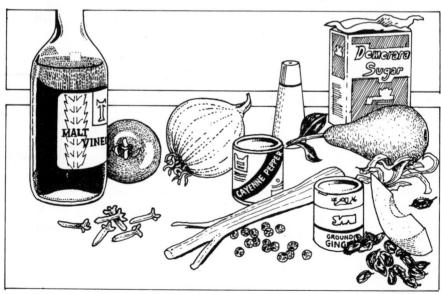

can be cut to size and used several times.

The muslin bag of spices added to chutneys when cooking should be removed before bottling.

Red Tomato Chutney

Ingredients

450g (1lb) onions
900ml (1½pt) malt vinegar
1.1kg (2½lb) ripe tomatoes
675g (1½lb) cooking apples
10ml (2 level tsp) salt
Good pinch of cayenne pepper
350g (¾lb) brown sugar
10ml (2 level tsp) ground ginger
50g (2oz) pickling spice
350g (¾lb) sultanas or chopped raisins

Peel and chop the onions finely and put into a preserving pan or large saucepan with half the vinegar and bring to the boil. Simmer gently until the onion is almost tender. Meanwhile peel the tomatoes (by first plunging into boiling water for 30 seconds then into cold water when the skins will split and peel off easily) and then chop. Peel, core and chop the apples finely. Add the tomatoes and apples to the pan with the remaining vinegar, salt, cayenne, sugar, ginger and sultanas. Tie the spices in a muslin bag and add to the chutney. Bring back to the boil slowly making sure the sugar has dissolved and then continue to cook slowly until thick and no liquid remains on the top, stirring occasionally to prevent burning. Remove bag of spices and pour chutney into hot jars. Seal whilst hot with a vinegar-proof cover and label. Cool and store in a cool dry place.

Tomato and Marrow Chutney

Ingredients

1.8kg (4lb) ripe tomatoes
450g (1lb) prepared marrow (ie peeled and seeds removed)
350g (¾lb) onions, peeled
15g (½oz) salt
5ml (1 level tsp) mixed spice
2.5ml (½ level tsp) paprika
25g (1oz) pickling spice
350g (¾lb) sugar
300ml (½pt) vinegar

Peel the tomatoes as for red tomato chutney and then slice thinly. Finely chop the marrow and onions and put into a preserving pan or large saucepan with the tomatoes. Stir in the salt, mixed spice and paprika and add the pickling spices tied in a muslin bag. Cook gently without any added liquid for about 1½ hours until very tender, stirring from time to time to prevent sticking. Dissolve the sugar in the vinegar and add to the chutney, mixing well. Continue to cook until the chutney becomes thick and there is no excess liquid on the top—about 20–30 minutes—again stirring occasionally to prevent sticking. Pour into hot jars and seal whilst hot with vinegar-proof covers. Label, cool and store in a cool dry place.

Note Either malt vinegar and brown sugar or white vinegar and white sugar can be used in this recipe.

Chutneys

Tomato and Date Chutney

Ingredients

900g (2lb) green tomatoes
450g (1lb) cooking apples
225–350g ($\frac{1}{2}$–$\frac{3}{4}$lb) stoned dates
450g (1lb) onions
225g ($\frac{1}{2}$lb) sultanas
600ml (1pt) vinegar
50g (2oz) salt
5ml (1 level tsp) ground ginger
3 cloves garlic, crushed
2.5ml ($\frac{1}{2}$ level tsp) whole cloves
2.5ml ($\frac{1}{2}$ level tsp) crushed allspice
5ml (1 level tsp) mustard seed
2–3 chillies
Piece of cinnamon stick
450g (1lb) brown sugar

Wipe the tomatoes and slice or chop; peel, core and chop the apples; chop the dates; and peel and finely chop the onions. Put all these vegetables into a preserving pan or large saucepan with the sultanas, vinegar (malt or white), salt, ginger and garlic. Tie the cloves, allspice, mustard seed, chillies and cinnamon stick in a muslin bag and add to the pan. Bring to the boil and simmer for about $\frac{3}{4}$ hour until tender, stirring occasionally. Add the sugar and heat gently until dissolved, then simmer until the chutney becomes thick and there is no extra liquid on the surface. Remove the bag of spices and pour the chutney into hot jars. Seal with a vinegar-proof cover, then label and store in a cool, dry place.

Note Red tomatoes can be used in this recipe in which case add the grated rind and juice of 1 lemon and cut the sugar to 350g ($\frac{3}{4}$lb).

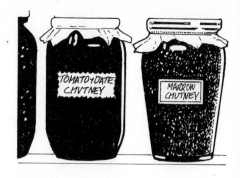

Marrow Chutney

Ingredients

1.4kg (3lb) prepared marrow (ie peeled and seeds removed)
50g (2oz) salt
225g ($\frac{1}{2}$lb) onions, peeled and chopped
350g ($\frac{3}{4}$lb) cooking apples, peeled and chopped
225g ($\frac{1}{2}$lb) sultanas or raisins
175g (6oz) demerara sugar
900ml (1$\frac{1}{2}$pt) malt vinegar
15ml (1 level tbsp) whole pickling spice
2–3 pieces root ginger, bruised

Cut the marrow into small dice and place in a bowl. Sprinkle with the salt, cover and leave to stand overnight. Rinse off the salt, drain the marrow thoroughly and put into a preserving pan or large saucepan. Add the onions, apples, sultanas, sugar and vinegar. Tie the spices and ginger in a muslin bag and add to the pan. Heat gently until the sugar has dissolved, stirring frequently, then bring to the boil and simmer gently until thick with no liquid on top. Stir occasionally. Remove the bag of spices and pour into hot jars. Seal whilst hot with vinegar-proof covers, label and store in a cool dry place.

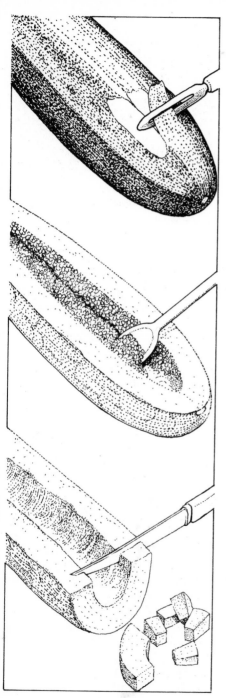

Green Tomato Chutney

Ingredients

1.8kg (4lb) green tomatoes
450g (1lb) cooking apples
350g (¾lb) onions, peeled
225g (½lb) sultanas
15g (½oz) salt
450g (1lb) brown sugar
750ml (1¼pt) vinegar
1 clove garlic, crushed
15ml (1 level tbsp) mustard seed
6 whole cloves
3 pieces root ginger, bruised
Good pinch of cayenne pepper
10ml (2 level tsp) curry powder
   (optional)

Wipe the tomatoes and remove stalks.
Peel, quarter and core the apples.
Coarsely mince the tomatoes, apples,
onions and sultanas and put into a
preserving pan or large saucepan with
the salt, sugar and vinegar. Tie the
garlic, mustard seed, cloves and ginger
in a muslin bag and add to the pan with
the cayenne and curry powder, if used.
Heat gently, stirring frequently, until
the sugar has dissolved and then cook
gently for about 2 hours or until thick
and pulpy with no extra liquid on the
top. Stir occasionally during cooking to
prevent sticking. Remove bag of spices
and pour the chutney into hot jars.
Seal whilst hot with a vinegar-proof
cover. Label and store in a cool dry
place.

Note If preferred the tomatoes, apples
and onions can be thinly sliced or
chopped and the sultanas can be left
whole.

Chutneys

Orchard Chutney

Ingredients

675g (1½lb) plums (freestone if
   possible)
900g (2lb) red tomatoes, peeled and
   sliced
900ml (1½pt) malt vinegar
15g (½oz) unpeeled garlic
450g (1lb) onions, peeled
1.1kg (2½lb) cooking apples, peeled
   and cored
225g (½lb) raisins
450g (1lb) demerara sugar
50g (2oz) salt
30ml (2 level tbsp) whole pickling
   spice

Wash the plums, cut in halves and
remove the stone if a freestone variety.
If not leave them whole. Put the plums,
tomatoes and vinegar into a preserving
pan or large saucepan and bring to the
boil. Simmer gently until the contents
are soft. Remove the plum stones if
they have not been removed. Peel the
garlic and mince it finely with the
onions, apples and dried fruit. Add to
the plum mixture and mix well, then
stir in the sugar and salt and the spices
tied in a muslin bag. Heat gently until
the sugar has dissolved, stirring
frequently and then bring to the boil
and simmer until everything is tender,
well reduced and thick—about 2 hours.
When all the liquid is absorbed pour
into hot jars and cover whilst hot with
vinegar-proof covers. Label and store
in a cool dry place.

Green Tomato and Pear Chutney

Ingredients

900g (2lb) green tomatoes
900g (2lb) pears
450g (1lb) onions
225g (½lb) celery
225g (½lb) raisins
2.5ml (½ level tsp) cayenne pepper
2.5ml (½ level tsp) ground ginger
10ml (2 level tsp) salt
1.1l (2pt) malt vinegar
12 whole peppercorns
4–5 whole cloves
675g (1½lb) demerara sugar

Wipe the tomatoes and slice thinly ;
peel, core and chop the pears ; peel and
finely chop the onion ; and finely chop
the celery. Put these ingredients into a
preserving pan or large saucepan with
all the other ingredients except the
sugar and with the peppercorns and
cloves tied in a muslin bag. Simmer
gently until soft—about ½ hour. Add the
sugar and stir until dissolved then
simmer until the chutney thickens and
excess liquid is absorbed. Pour into hot
jars, seal with a vinegar-proof cover,
label and store in a cool, dry place.

Beetroot Chutney

Ingredients

1.1kg (2½lb) cooked beetroot
225g (½lb) onions
450g (1lb) cooking apples
225g (½lb) raisins
15g (½oz) salt
225g (½lb) brown sugar
600ml (1pt) malt vinegar
15ml (1 level tbsp) whole pickling
   spice
4 whole cloves

Peel the beetroot and chop finely. Peel and chop or mince the onions, apples and raisins and put into a preserving pan or large saucepan with the salt, sugar, vinegar and spices tied in a muslin bag. Heat gently until the sugar has dissolved and then bring to the boil and simmer until the onion is tender and the mixture thickened. Add the beetroot and continue until thick and well blended and there is no excess liquid on the surface. This should take about $\frac{1}{2}$ hour. Remove the bag of spices and pour the chutney into hot jars. Seal whilst hot with vinegar-proof covers and then label and store in a cool dry place.

Pepper Chutney

Ingredients

6 red peppers
6 green peppers
900g (2lb) green tomatoes
450g (1lb) onions, peeled
450g (1lb) cooking apples, peeled and cored
450g (1lb) sugar
25g (1oz) salt
2.5ml ($\frac{1}{2}$ level tsp) ground pepper
900ml (1$\frac{1}{2}$pt) vinegar
50g (2oz) whole pickling spice
2–3 pieces root ginger, bruised
6 cloves

Deseed the peppers and discard with the stems and then mince the flesh coarsely with the tomatoes, onions and apples. Put into a preserving pan or large saucepan with the sugar, salt, pepper and vinegar. Tie the spices, ginger and cloves in a muslin bag and add to the pan. Heat gently until the sugar has dissolved, stirring frequently. Bring to the boil and simmer for 2–3

hours or until the chutney is thick with no extra liquid on the surface. Remove the bag of spices and pour the chutney into hot jars. Seal with a vinegar-proof cover while still hot. Label jars and store in a cool dry place.

Pumpkin Chutney

Ingredients

675g (2$\frac{1}{2}$lb) prepared pumpkin (ie peeled and seeds removed)
350g ($\frac{3}{4}$lb) onions
225g ($\frac{1}{2}$lb) ripe tomatoes
350g ($\frac{3}{4}$lb) cooking apples
175g (6oz) sultanas
30ml (2 level tbsp) salt
10ml (2 level tsp) ground ginger
2.5ml ($\frac{1}{2}$ level tsp) ground black pepper
10ml (2 level tsp) ground allspice
4 cloves garlic, crushed
600ml (1pt) malt vinegar
450g (1lb) brown sugar

Finely chop the pumpkin ; peel and finely chop the onions and tomatoes ; and peel, core and chop the apples. Place these ingredients in a preserving pan or large saucepan with all the other ingredients except the sugar and bring to the boil. Simmer gently for about $\frac{3}{4}$ hour or until soft, stirring occasionally. Stir in the sugar until dissolved and then continue to simmer for 1–1$\frac{1}{2}$ hours, until the chutney is very thick and with no extra liquid on the surface. Stir fairly frequently as it thickens to prevent sticking or burning. Pour the chutney into hot jars and seal whilst hot with vinegar-proof covers and then label and store in a cool dry place.

Chutneys

Rhubarb Chutney

Ingredients

2.3kg (5lb) rhubarb, trimmed
450g (1lb) onions
900ml (1½pt) vinegar
Grated rind of 1 large lemon
15g (½oz) salt
15g (½oz) ground ginger
25g (1oz) ground mixed spice
10ml (2 level tsp) ground cinnamon
1–2 cloves garlic, crushed
900g (2lb) sugar

Wash the rhubarb and cut into 1.5cm (½in) lengths. Peel and mince the onions, or chop finely if preferred. Put the rhubarb and onions into a preserving pan or large saucepan with 300ml (½pt) vinegar, the lemon rind, salt and spices. Bring to the boil and simmer gently until the rhubarb is mushy. Add the remaining vinegar and sugar, heat gently until the sugar has dissolved, stirring frequently ; and then boil the chutney until it is thick with no liquid on top. Stir occasionally to prevent sticking. Pour into hot jars, seal with vinegar-proof covers whilst hot and label. Store in a cool dry place.

Rhubarb and Ginger Chutney

Follow the above recipe but increase the ground ginger to 25g (1oz) or more to taste and, if available, add 50–100g (2–3oz) very finely chopped stem or crystallized ginger with the remaining vinegar and sugar.

Pear Chutney

Ingredients

1.4kg (3lb) pears
450g (1lb) onions
450g (1lb) ripe tomatoes
1 small pepper, red or green
225g ($\frac{1}{2}$lb) sultanas
450g (1lb) demerara sugar
15g ($\frac{1}{2}$oz) salt
1.25ml ($\frac{1}{4}$ level tsp) cayenne pepper
2.5ml ($\frac{1}{2}$ level tsp) ground ginger
1.1l (2 pt) malt vinegar
8 peppercorns
4 whole cloves

Peel, core and finely chop the pears ; peel and finely chop or mince the onions ; peel and slice the tomatoes and deseed and chop the pepper. Place these ingredients in a preserving pan or large saucepan, cover and cook gently without any extra added liquid until soft, stirring from time to time. Put the sugar, salt, cayenne, ginger and vinegar into a pan and heat gently until the sugar dissolves then add to the softened mixture. Tie the peppercorns and cloves in a muslin bag, add to the pan and bring up to the boil. Simmer, uncovered, until the chutney becomes thick without any liquid on the top. Remove the muslin bag, pour into hot jars and seal with vinegar-proof covers as usual. Label and store in a cool dry place.

Peach Chutney

Ingredients

900g (2lb) peaches
450g (1lb) onions, peeled and chopped
175g (6oz) raisins
225g ($\frac{1}{2}$lb) soft brown sugar
300ml ($\frac{1}{2}$pt) vinegar
Grated rind and juice of 1 lemon
Grated rind and juice of 1 small orange
5ml (1 level tsp) salt
5ml (1 level tsp) dry mustard
5ml (1 level tsp) ground ginger
Good pinch of chilli powder
Piece of cinnamon stick

Wash the peaches, remove skins if liked by plunging first into boiling water for $\frac{1}{2}$ minute and then into cold water when they should rub off easily. Remove stones and slice the fruit and then place it in a preserving pan or large saucepan with the onions, raisins, sugar, vinegar and all the remaining ingredients. Heat gently until the sugar has dissolved, stirring frequently ; then bring to the boil. Simmer uncovered, until the chutney becomes thick and there is no liquid on the top, stirring occasionally to prevent sticking and burning. Remove the cinnamon stick and pour chutney into hot jars. Seal whilst hot with a vinegar-proof cover and label. Store in a cool dry place.

Note Unripe peaches can be used for this recipe in which case increase the sugar content to 450g (1lb). Also cheap damaged peaches can be used if weighed after cutting out all the bad and blemished parts of the fruit.

Chutneys

Plum Chutney

Ingredients

1.4kg (3lb) plums
450g (1lb) cooking apples
225g ($\frac{1}{2}$lb) carrots
225g ($\frac{1}{2}$lb) onions
1.1l (2pt) vinegar
225g ($\frac{1}{2}$lb) raisins
40g (1$\frac{1}{2}$oz) salt
5ml (1 level tsp) ground cloves
10ml (2 level tsp) ground cinnamon
10 ml (2 level tsp) ground ginger
10ml (2 level tsp) ground allspice
450g (1lb) sugar

Wash the plums and remove the stalks and any blemished parts of the fruit. Cut into quarters and remove the stones. Peel and core the apples, peel the carrots and the onions and either chop finely, mince or grate these three ingredients. Put the plums into a preserving pan or large saucepan with the apples, carrots and onions and half the vinegar. Bring to the boil and simmer gently until everything is very tender. Add the remaining ingredients and heat gently until the sugar has dissolved. Bring to the boil and simmer until the chutney is thick and with no extra liquid on the surface. Pour into hot jars and seal whilst hot with vinegar-proof covers. Label and store in a cool dry place.

Note Malt vinegar and brown sugar will give a richer darker chutney than white sugar and white vinegar and the colour of the plums used will also vary the colour.

Variations Cider vinegar can be used in place of half or all the vinegar ; the carrots can be omitted ; and sultanas can be used in place of raisins. For a hotter chutney tie 4–5 chillies in a muslin bag and add 5–10ml (1–2 level tsp) curry powder.

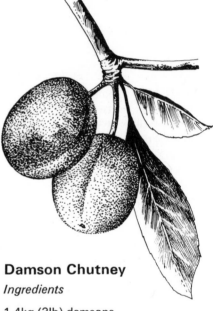

Damson Chutney

Ingredients

1.4kg (3lb) damsons
450g (1lb) cooking apples
350g ($\frac{3}{4}$lb) onions
225g ($\frac{1}{2}$lb) raisins
450g (1lb) brown sugar
900ml (1$\frac{1}{2}$pt) vinegar
7.5ml (1$\frac{1}{2}$ level tsp) salt
2.5ml ($\frac{1}{2}$ level tsp) ground allspice
20g ($\frac{3}{4}$oz) ground ginger
2 cloves garlic, crushed (optional)

Wash the damsons ; peel, core and chop the apples ; peel and chop the onions and chop the raisins. Put in a preserving pan or large saucepan with all the other ingredients. Heat gently until the sugar has dissolved, stirring frequently, then bring to the boil. Simmer for about 1½ hours, removing the damson stones as they rise to the surface, until the chutney is thick and without any extra liquid on the surface. Remove any more visible damson stones and then pour the hot chutney into hot jars. Seal at once with vinegar-proof covers then label jars and store in a cool dry place.

Note Purple plums can be used in place of the damsons and 2.5–5ml (½–1 level tsp) dry mustard and 1.25–2.5ml (¼–½ level tsp) cayenne can be added to give a hotter chutney. White vinegar and sugar give a brighter chutney whilst brown sugar and malt vinegar give a richer, darker chutney.

Blackberry Chutney

Ingredients

450g (1lb) cooking apples
1.4kg (3lb) blackberries
450g (1lb) onions
20g (¾oz) salt
25g (1oz) dry mustard
25g (1oz) ground ginger
5ml (1 level tsp) ground mace
5ml (1 level tsp) cayenne pepper
600ml (1pt) vinegar
450g (1lb) brown sugar

Peel, core and chop the apples and put into a preserving pan or large saucepan with the blackberries and peeled and finely chopped onions. Add all the remaining ingredients except the sugar and bring to the boil. Simmer for about 1 hour or until everything is soft and mushy. Rub the chutney through a nylon sieve to remove all the pips and put in a clean pan. Add the sugar and

heat gently until it has dissolved. Bring back to the boil and simmer until thick with no extra liquid on the surface. Pour the chutney into hot jars and seal with vinegar-proof covers. Label jars and store in a cool dry place.

Chutneys

Gooseberry Chutney

Ingredients

1.4kg (3lb) gooseberries
225g ($\frac{1}{2}$lb) onions, peeled
225g ($\frac{1}{2}$lb) raisins or sultanas
450g (1lb) sugar, brown or white
300ml ($\frac{1}{2}$pt) water
15g ($\frac{1}{2}$oz) salt
15ml (1 level tbsp) ground ginger
2.5ml ($\frac{1}{2}$ level tsp) cayenne pepper
600ml (1pt) vinegar, malt or white

Wash the gooseberries and top and tail. Either roughly cut up the gooseberries and chop the onions finely or, for a smoother chutney, mince the gooseberries, onions and raisins. Put into a preserving pan or large saucepan with the water and simmer gently until soft and mushy. Add all the other ingredients and heat gently until the sugar has dissolved, then bring to the boil and simmer until the chutney becomes thick and there is no extra liquid on the surface. Pour the chutney into hot jars and seal whilst still hot with vinegar-proof covers. Label and store in a cool dry place.

Note For a variation use half tarragon vinegar and half malt or white vinegar. Brown sugar and malt vinegar will give a richer darker coloured chutney than white vinegar and white sugar.

Apple and Onion Chutney

Ingredients

1.4kg (3lb) cooking apples
1.4kg (3lb) onions
1–2 green peppers
225g ($\frac{1}{2}$lb) sultanas
Grated rind and juice of 2 lemons
600ml (1pt) malt vinegar
25g (1oz) whole pickling spice
675g (1$\frac{1}{2}$lb) demerara sugar

Peel, core and chop the apples ; peel and finely chop or mince the onions and deseed and finely chop or mince the peppers. Place in a preserving pan or large saucepan with the sultanas, grated rind and juice of the lemons, vinegar and pickling spices tied in a muslin bag. Bring to the boil and simmer for $\frac{1}{2}$ hour. Stir in the sugar heating gently until dissolved and then bring back to the boil and simmer until the chutney is thick and with no extra liquid on the surface. Remove the bag of spices and pour into hot jars. Seal whilst hot with vinegar-proof covers, label the jars and store in a cool dry place.

Apple Chutney

Ingredients

1.4kg (3lb) cooking apples
450g (1lb) onions
150ml ($\frac{1}{4}$pt) water
350g ($\frac{3}{4}$lb) white sugar
225g ($\frac{1}{2}$lb) golden syrup
100g (4oz) dates or raisins, chopped
20g ($\frac{3}{4}$oz) ground ginger
10ml (2 level tsp) ground cinnamon
3 chillies (tied in muslin)
5ml (1 level tsp) ground allspice
20g ($\frac{3}{4}$oz) salt
600ml (1pt) white vinegar

Peel and core the apples and either chop or coarsely mince. Peel the onions and finely chop or mince. Put apples, onions and water in a pan, cover and simmer for about 20 minutes or until soft. Add the remaining ingredients and heat gently until the sugar and syrup have dissolved. Mix well and bring to the boil. Simmer until the chutney becomes thick with no extra liquid on the surface. Remove the

chillies and pour into hot jars. Seal whilst still hot with vinegar-proof covers and label. Store in a cool dry place.

Indian Style Chutney

Ingredients

900g (2lb) cooking apples
225g ($\frac{1}{2}$lb) onions
2–3 large cloves garlic, crushed
900ml (1$\frac{1}{2}$pt) malt vinegar
450g (1lb) dark soft brown sugar
225g ($\frac{1}{2}$lb) raisins, chopped
75–100g (3–4oz) stem or crystallized
  ginger, chopped
10ml (2 level tsp) salt
15ml (1 level tbsp) dry mustard
2.5ml ($\frac{1}{2}$ level tsp) cayenne pepper
2.5ml ($\frac{1}{2}$ level tsp) ground allspice

Peel, core and slice the apples and put into a preserving pan or large saucepan with the peeled and finely chopped or minced onions. Add the garlic and vinegar and bring to the boil. Simmer gently until the mixture is soft and reduced to a pulp. The mixture can be liquidized or sieved at this stage to give a really smooth texture if liked. Add the remaining ingredients, heating gently until the sugar has dissolved then simmer for about $\frac{1}{2}$–$\frac{3}{4}$ hour or until the chutney becomes thick and without any excess liquid on the surface. Pour into hot jars and seal with vinegar-proof covers. Label jars and store in a cool dry place for 2–3 months before using.

Jams

Jams are a most rewarding preserve to make for they will use up any glut of fruit you may have in your garden or get hold of cheaply. A good jam should be clear and bright, with a good colour, be well set but not too stiff, with a good flavour and must keep well. To help achieve this result, first use a heavy preserving pan, where possible made from heavy aluminium, stainless steel or enamel-lined. Old-fashioned unlined copper or brass pans can be used for jams, jellies and marmalades (but not chutneys because of the vinegar) but they must be properly cleaned and any tarnishes or discolourations removed with a special cleaner before use ; and they will destroy some of the vitamin C content of the jam ; also do not leave the preserve to stand around in this type of pan for long. A thick base is necessary for jams tend to burn after the sugar is added ; a wide top is necessary to help with the evaporation of water during cooking and it must be deep enough to prevent boiling over. A large saucepan can be used if a preserving pan is not available but the cooking time may be a little longer for the narrower top will cut down the speed of evaporation.

It is an idea to keep a large wooden spoon especially for jam making (and another for chutneys) for they become discoloured easily but are better than metal spoons. A slotted spoon is also good for removing scum from the surface and also for removing stones from jams such as damson when it is not possible to remove them before cooking. Any sieves used should be made of nylon.

A good supply of clean and sound jam jars is necessary. The sizes can vary to suit your own needs but 450g (1 lb) and 900g (2lb) are the most useful. Wash well in warm soapy water, rinse and dry before use. Then before potting the jam put the jars into a warm oven to heat up. Pouring hot jam into cold jars will break them and waste the jam. Commercial covers are sold in packets containing waxed discs (remember wax side touching the jam), cellophane covers, rubber bands and labels.

Fruit used for jam should be sound and ripe or just underripe—if overripe fruit is used the pectin content may be rather low. Pectin is the absolute necessity in fruit to set the jam with the addition of sugar and acid. Some fruits are rich in pectin and acid ie cooking apples, red and blackcurrants, gooseberries, damsons, Seville oranges, lemons and limes which easily give a good setting jam ; apricots, loganberries, raspberries, most plums and gages have a reasonable content but strawberries, cherries, pears, marrows and rhubarb have only a low content and need a helping hand with the addition of lemon juice or a high pectin fruit juice ie redcurrant juice. Lemon juice is the most often used for it not only aids the setting but often brings out the flavour of the fruit. Allow 30ml (2tbsp) lemon juice to 1.8kg (4lb) fruit with poor setting qualities. A commercial pectin is available from chemists and can also be used following the manufacturer's directions or you can make your own pectin extract (see below). In some cases only extra acid (tartaric or citric acid) is required to help extract the pectin from the fruit tissues and bring out the flavour. Use 2.5ml ($\frac{1}{2}$ level tsp) per 1.8kg (4lb) fruit.

Home-made Pectin Extract

Take 900g (2lb) fruit (sour cooking apples, crab apples, redcurrants, gooseberries, apple peelings or windfalls) and cut it up without peeling or coring. Put into a pan with 600–900ml (1–1$\frac{1}{2}$pt) water. Stew gently for about $\frac{3}{4}$ hour or until well broken down and mushy. Strain through a jelly bag and use 150–300ml ($\frac{1}{4}$–$\frac{1}{2}$pt) of this juice to 1.8kg (4lb) fruit that is low in pectin.

Sugar is essential for jam making and the type used can be granulated, lump or preserving crystals. Granulated will cause more scum on top of the jams but is the cheapest. Add the sugar after the fruit has been cooked and is quite tender with the contents of the pan well reduced in volume. Remove from the heat and stir in until dissolved before reheating or the sugar will burn and spoil the jam. Too little sugar added will cause the jam to ferment whilst too much will cause crystallization during storage. A knob of butter added after the sugar has dissolved will help to prevent foaming and the resulting scum forming on the surface.

To test the jam for a set is very important for whilst under-boiled jam will not set, over boiling will make it too stiff and lose volume. There are three main ways of testing. The easiest and most accurate method is with a sugar thermometer. The warmed thermometer is placed in the jam when the sugar has dissolved and when it reaches 105°C (221°F), a set should be obtained. There are some fruits which are ready 1° lower or need 1° more but this can be double checked by using one of the other methods as well. For the flake test remove some jam on a wooden spoon and then let the jam drop off. If it has been boiled long enough, the drops will run together to form flakes which will then break off sharply. The saucer test is very simple— put a little jam on a cold saucer and leave it to cool. Push your finger across the jam when it should wrinkle. Remember to remove jam from the heat whilst doing this or it may overcook. Return jam to the pan and continue a little longer if it does not wrinkle.

Once setting point is reached pour the hot jam straight away into warmed jars filling them right up to the neck. However, with whole fruit jams such as strawberry, and marmalades, the jam must be left to stand for up to 15 minutes before potting to prevent the fruit rising in the jars. Cover with a waxed disc whilst hot—wax side downwards—making sure it lies flat to come in contact with the jam. Either cover at once with a dampened cellophane round secured with a rubber band or leave until cold before doing so. Hot or cold covering is a matter of preference. Label jars and store in a cool, dark and dry place.

Jams

Strawberry Jam (1)

Ingredients

1.6kg (3½lb) strawberries
45ml (3tbsp) lemon juice
1.4kg (3lb) sugar

Hull the strawberries and wipe over any which are dirty. It is better not to wash unless absolutely necessary. Put the fruit into a preserving pan with the lemon juice and heat very gently in their own juice until really soft—about 30 minutes, stirring frequently. Add the sugar and stir until dissolved and bring up to the boil. Boil hard without further stirring until setting point is reached, 105°C (221°F). Remove any scum from the surface then leave the jam to stand for about 15 minutes to prevent the fruit rising in the jars. Pour into clean warmed jars and cover whilst hot with wax discs and then with a

dampened cellophane circle. Leave to cool, label and store in a cool, dark place. Approx yield : 2.3kg (5lb).

Strawberry Jam (2)

Ingredients

1.8kg (4lb) strawberries
900g (2lb) redcurrants or 15ml (1 level tbsp) citric or tartaric acid
1.8kg (4lb) sugar

If using redcurrants, wash them carefully and put into a saucepan with about 150ml (¼pt) water. Simmer gently till very tender, mash well and either pass through a very fine sieve or strain through a jelly bag to obtain the juice. Hull the strawberries and wipe any that are dirty. Wash only if absolutely necessary. Put into a preserving pan with the redcurrant juice and bring to the boil. Simmer gently until very tender then stir in the sugar until dissolved. Boil rapidly, without stirring for about 15 minutes or until setting point is reached, 105°C (221°F). Cool for about 15 minutes to prevent the fruit rising and cover whilst hot with waxed discs and then with a dampened cellophane circle. Leave to cool, label and store in a cool, dark place. Approx yield : 3.2kg (7lb).

Note Strawberries are low in pectin content and need either lemon juice or an acid to aid the setting. If using acid, make the jam as for Strawberry Jam (1), adding the acid to the pan with the strawberries.

Raspberry Jam (1)

Ingredients

1.8kg (4lb) fresh raspberries
1.8kg (4lb) sugar

Hull the fruit, look over carefully and wash only if necessary. Put into a preserving pan with no extra water and heat gently until the juice begins to run, and then simmer in its own juice for about 15–20 minutes or until really soft. Stir in the sugar until dissolved and then bring back to the boil and boil rapidly until setting point is reached, 105°C (221°F). Pour into warmed jars, cover with a wax disc and then with a dampened cellophane circle. Cool, label and store in a cool, dark place. Approx yield : 2.3kg (5lb).

Raspberry Jam (2)

Ingredients

2.3kg (5lb) fresh raspberries
2.7kg (6lb) sugar

Look over the fruit carefully and wash only if necessary. Place in a preserving pan with no added water. Simmer very gently until the juice begins to flow and then bring to the boil and boil for 10 minutes. Warm the sugar in a low oven and stir into the raspberries until dissolved. Bring back to the boil quickly and boil rapidly for 2 minutes. Pour into warmed jars, cover whilst hot with a waxed disc and then with a dampened cellophane circle. Cool, label and store in a cool, dark place. Approx yield : 4.5kg (10lb).

Note This jam does not set very firmly but has a good colour and a really fresh-fruit flavour.

Blackcurrant Jam

Ingredients

1.8kg (4lb) blackcurrants
1.7l (3pt) water
2.7kg (6lb) sugar

Remove the stalks from the fruit and then wash carefully. Drain fruit well and put into a preserving pan with the water. Bring to the boil and simmer gently until the fruit is soft and the contents of the pan well reduced. If the fruit is still tough at this stage the finished jam will still remain tough, so take care to cook sufficiently. Add the sugar and stir until it has dissolved. Bring back to the boil and boil rapidly until setting point is reached 105°C (221°F). Remove any scum from the surface then pour into warmed jars. Cover with waxed discs and a dampened cellophane circle. Cool, label and store in a cool, dark place. Approx yield : 4.5kg (10lb).

Jams

Gooseberry and Strawberry Jam

Ingredients

900g (2lb) ripe gooseberries
450ml (¾pt) water
900g (2lb) strawberries
1.8kg (4lb) sugar

Top and tail the gooseberries and wash well. Put into a preserving pan with the water, bring to the boil and simmer until soft. Add the hulled and wiped strawberries and cook for a further 20–30 minutes until tender but not overcooked. Stir in the sugar until dissolved then boil rapidly until setting point is reached—about 20 minutes. 105°C (221°F). Cool for about 15 minutes then pour into hot jars. Cover with waxed discs and then a dampened cellophane circle. Cool, label and store in a cool, dark place. Approx yield: 2.3–2.7kg (5–6lb).

Note This jam has an excellent flavour and the acidity of the gooseberries gives the strawberries the pectin needed for a good set.

Gooseberry Jam

Ingredients

1.8kg (4lb) gooseberries
750ml (1¼pt) water
2.3kg (5lb) sugar

The colour of the finished jam will depend on the type of fruit used and its maturity as well as the length of boiling after adding the sugar. Longer boiling gives a deeper red colour but to get the greenest jam use a copper or brass pan for the cooking.

Top and tail the gooseberries and wash. Drain well and put into a preserving pan with the water and bring to the boil. Simmer gently until the fruit is quite tender (if the skins are tough at this point they will still be so in the finished jam) and the contents of the pan well reduced. Add the sugar and stir until dissolved. Bring back to the boil and boil rapidly until setting point is reached, 105°C (221°F). Remove scum from the surface and then pour into warmed jars. Cover with a waxed disc and then a dampened cellophane circle. Cool, label and store in a cool, dark place. Approx yield: 4.5kg (10lb).

Note For a pleasant variation add 14–16 well washed heads of elderflowers (tied in a muslin bag) to the pan with the gooseberres and water. Before adding the sugar, remove the bag, squeezing out all the juice and continue as above.

Pumpkin Jam

Ingredients

1.4kg (3lb) prepared pumpkin (ie
    peeled and seeds removed)
900ml–1.1l (1½–2pt) water
50g (2oz) root ginger, bruised or
    7.5ml (1½ level tsp) ground ginger
Grated rind of 2 lemons (optional)
Juice of 2 lemons
1.4kg (3lb) sugar
50–75g (2–3oz) preserved ginger,
    finely chopped (optional)

Cut the pumpkin into small dice and
put into a preserving pan with the water
and ginger (tie root ginger in a muslin
bag). Bring to the boil, cover and
simmer very gently until the pumpkin
is mushy and very tender. Remove
from the heat and mash thoroughly.
Stir in the lemon rind (if used) and
juice and the sugar until dissolved.
Bring back to the boil and boil rapidly
until setting point is reached, 105°C
(221°F), stirring occasionally as the
jam will be very thick and tends to
stick. Remove the bag of ginger, then
stir in the chopped ginger, if used, and
pour the jam into warmed jars. Cover
with a waxed disc and then a
dampened cellophane circle. Cool,
label and store in a cool, dark place.
Approx yield: 2kg (4½lb).

Marrow Jam

Ingredients

2.3kg (5lb) prepared marrow (ie
    peeled and seeds removed)
Finely grated rind and juice of 3 large
    lemons
50g (2oz) root ginger, bruised or
    7.5ml (1½ level tsp) ground ginger
2.3kg (5lb) sugar

There are two methods of making this
jam:

Method 1   Cut the marrow into cubes
about 1cm (½in) square. Place in a
steamer and steam gently until just
tender, then put into a bowl with the
grated rinds and juice of the lemons and
the bruised ginger tied in a muslin bag.
Add the sugar and leave to stand in a
covered bowl for 24 hours. Transfer to a
preserving pan and heat gently until all
the sugar has dissolved, stirring
frequently. Bring to the boil and cook
until the marrow is transparent and the
syrup thick and continue until setting
point is reached, 105°C (221°F).
Remove the bag of ginger and any
scum on the surface and leave to stand
for 5–10 minutes. Pour into warmed
jars, cover with waxed discs and a
dampened cellophane circle. Cool,
label and store in a cool, dark, place.
Approx yield: 3.4kg (7½lb).

Method 2   Place the cubed marrow
(as above) in a bowl with about 450g
(1lb) sugar and leave to stand
overnight in a covered bowl. The next
day put the lemon juice and rinds,
bruised ginger tied in a muslin bag and
the marrow into a preserving pan and
bring slowly to the boil. Simmer gently
for about ½ hour, then stir in the
remaining sugar and return to the boil.
Continue to boil fairly gently until the
marrow becomes transparent, the
syrup is thick and setting point is
reached. Remove the muslin bag and
pot and cover as above.

Jams

Rhubarb and Ginger Jam

Ingredients

1.4kg (3lb) prepared rhubarb
1.4kg (3lb) sugar
Juice of 2 lemons
Grated rind of 1 lemon (optional)
25g (1oz) root ginger, bruised
50–75g (2–3oz) preserved or
    crystallized ginger, finely chopped
    (optional)

Wash the rhubarb, drain well and cut into small chunks. Put into a bowl layered up with the sugar and lemon juice and cover bowl. Leave to stand overnight. The next day transfer this mixture to a preserving pan adding the lemon rind, if used, and root ginger tied in a muslin bag. Bring slowly to the boil, stirring frequently until the sugar has dissolved. Boil rapidly for 15 minutes then remove the muslin bag, and add the chopped ginger, if used. Continue to boil until the rhubarb is transparent and setting point is reached, 105°C (221°F). Remove any scum from the surface and pour into warmed jars. Cover with waxed discs and then with a dampened cellophane circle. Cool, label and store in a cool, dark place. Approx yield : 2.3kg (5lb).

Rhubarb and Lemon Jam

Make as above but omit both the root and preserved ginger and use the finely grated rind of 3 lemons and 2.5–5ml (½–1 level tsp) ground mixed spice.

Rhubarb and Raspberry Jam

Ingredients

1.8kg (4lb) prepared rhubarb
300ml (½pt) water
900g (2lb) raspberries
2.7kg (6lb) sugar

Wash the rhubarb and drain well and cut into small chunks. Put into a pan with the water and bring to the boil, cover and simmer until tender and mushy. Remove the lid, add the raspberries and continue to simmer until the fruit is tender and the contents of the pan reduced. Add the sugar, stirring continuously until dissolved and then bring back to the boil. Boil rapidly until setting point is reached, 105°C (221°F). Remove any scum from the surface and pour into warmed jars. Cover with waxed discs and a

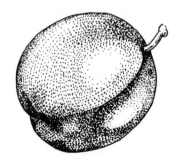

dampened cellophane circle. Cool, label and store in a cool, dark place. Approx yield : 4.5kg (10lb).

Note Loganberries, if available, can be used in place of raspberries. The softer and slightly damaged raspberries unsuitable for freezing can be used for this recipe.

Plum Jam

Ingredients

2.7kg (6lb) plums
300–900ml ($\frac{1}{2}$–1$\frac{1}{2}$pt) water
2.7kg (6lb) sugar

Remove stalks from the fruit then wash and drain well. Cut the plums in halves and remove the stones. Crack some stones and remove the kernels, if liked. If the plums are not the freestone variety leave them whole. Put the plums and kernels into a preserving pan with the water and bring to the boil. Simmer gently until the fruit is very soft and the contents of the pan well reduced. (If using whole fruit remove the stones as they rise to the surface with a slotted spoon.) Add the sugar and stir until well dissolved then bring to the boil. Boil rapidly until setting point is reached, 105°C (221 °F), remove any scum from the surface and pour into warm jars. Cover with waxed discs and a dampened cellophane circle. Cool, label and store in a cool, dark place. Approx yield : 4.5kg (10lb).

Note: Dark coloured plums will obviously give a richer darker finished jam than the lighter varieties. Green and yellow gages when available can be used in this way to make jams.

The amount of water used depends on the juiciness of the fruit and also on the fruit content required in the finished jam. Use less water with very juicy plums and gages and more with the drier varieties.

Cherry Jam

Ingredients

1.8kg (4lb) cherries (Morello or May Duke are best)
Juice of 3 lemons or 7.5ml (1$\frac{1}{2}$ level tsp) tartaric or citric acid
1.6kg (3$\frac{1}{2}$lb) sugar

Wash and stone the cherries and put the fruit into a preserving pan. Crack a few of the stones and remove the kernels to add to the pan with the lemon juice or acid. Bring to the boil slowly and simmer very gently until the fruit is really tender, stirring occasionally to prevent sticking. Add the sugar and stir until dissolved, then bring back to the boil and boil rapidly until setting point is reached, 105°C (221 °F). Remove any scum from the surface, pour into warmed jars, cover with waxed discs and then with dampened cellophane circles. Cool, label and store in a cool, dark place. Approx yield : 2.3kg (5lb).

Note Cherries are low in pectin and consequently this jam has only a light set, but the flavour is very good. A firmer setting jam needs a fruit such as redcurrants or gooseberries added to supply the lacking pectin. Use 900g (2lb) cherries, 450g (1lb) redcurrants or other fruit, 150ml ($\frac{1}{4}$pt) water and 1.4kg (3lb) sugar and make as for blackcurrant jam (see p 37) cooking the cherries and other fruit together.

Jams

Fig Jam

Ingredients

675g (1½lb) fresh green figs
350–450g (¾–1lb) tart cooking apples
Finely grated rind of 2 lemons
Juice of 4 lemons
675g (1½lb) sugar

Wash the figs and remove stalks, then slice. Peel, core and slice the apples and put into a pan with the prepared figs, lemon rind and juice. Bring to the boil, cover pan and cook very gently, stirring from time to time, until the figs are very tender. (If the figs are tough at this stage they will remain tough in the finished jam.) Add the sugar and stir until dissolved then bring back to the boil and boil rapidly for 15 minutes. Continue to boil until setting point is reached, 105°C (221°F). Remove any scum from the surface, pour into warmed jars and cover first with waxed discs and then a dampened cellophane circle. Cool, label and store in a cool, dark place. Approx yield : 900g (2lb).

Rose Petal Jam (1)

This is an unusual, novelty jam with a strong, distinctive flavour. Use thin-petalled roses where possible when they are full blown for the best results—and use it sparingly.

Ingredients

450g (1lb) rose petals
675g (1½lb) sugar
300ml (½pt) water
Juice of half lemon

Pick the petals when they are dry from full blown roses and then cut off the white base of each petal. Cut petals into uneven pieces and place in a bowl with half the sugar. Mix well, cover bowl and leave to stand in a cool place for 48 hours. Dissolve the remaining sugar slowly in the water in a pan without boiling and then add the lemon juice and rose petal mixture (which will have darkened in colour and have a very strong scent). Bring up to the boil and simmer gently for about 15–20 minutes until the jam thickens then continue until setting point is reached, 105°C (221°F). Remove any scum from the surface and cool for a few minutes before pouring into warmed jars. Cover with waxed discs and a dampened cellophane circle. Cool, label and store in a cool dark place. Approx yield : 900g (2lb).

Rose Petal Jam (2)

Ingredients

100g (4oz) rose petals
675g (1½lb) sugar
15ml (1tbsp) lemon juice
150ml (¼pt) rose water
150ml (¼pt) water

Prepare the rose petals as for recipe above then put into a bowl. Dissolve the sugar with the lemon juice, rose water and water in a pan over a gentle heat, stirring continuously, then bring to the boil and simmer for 5 minutes. Pour over the petals, mix well, cover bowl and leave to stand overnight. The next day turn the rose petal mixture into a saucepan and bring up to the boil. Simmer gently, stirring continuously, for about 30 minutes until the syrup thickens and setting point is reached, 105 °C (221 °F). Continue as above.

Rosehip and Apple Jam

Another unusual preserve making use of the hedgerow rosehips and apples which can be windfalls if they are weighed after cutting out bad and bruised parts of the fruit.

Ingredients

900g (2lb) ripe rosehips
1.7l (3pt) water
900g (2lb) tart cooking apples
725–900g (1$\frac{3}{4}$–2lb) sugar

Wash the rosehips thoroughly and drain. Put into a pan with the water, bring to the boil, cover and simmer until very soft and pulpy. Strain through a jelly bag overnight. Peel, core and chop the apples and put into a pan with the very minimum of water and cook gently in a covered pan until a soft pulp. Stir occasionally to prevent sticking. Add the rosehip juice and the

sugar and stir until the sugar has dissolved. Bring up to the boil and boil rapidly until setting point is reached, 105 °C (221 °F). Remove any scum from the surface and pour at once into warmed jars. Cover with waxed discs and a dampened cellophane circle and cool, label and store in a cool, dark place. Approx yield : 1.6kg (3$\frac{1}{2}$lb).

Quince Jam

When available, quinces make a most delicious jam.

Ingredients

900g (2lb) quinces
225g ($\frac{1}{2}$lb) apples
900ml (1$\frac{1}{2}$pt) water
1.4kg (3lb) sugar

Wash the fruit well then peel, core and finely chop the flesh. Put all the peelings and cores into a pan with the roughly chopped up apples (including peel and cores) and the water. Bring to the boil, cover and simmer gently until pulpy. Strain the juice through a jelly bag then replace in a clean saucepan. Add the chopped quince flesh and simmer gently until quite tender but still in cubes, and the contents of the pan are reduced by about one-third. Add the sugar and stir until dissolved, then bring to the boil and boil rapidly until setting point is reached, 105 °C (221 °F). Remove any scum from the surface and leave to stand for 15 minutes before potting to prevent the fruit rising. Pour into warmed jars, cover with waxed discs and then a dampened cellophane circle. Cool, label and store in a cool, dark place. Approx yield : 2.3kg (5lb).

Jellies

The same principles apply to jelly making as to jam making with a few extra considerations, and as with jam, to get the correct set of the jelly there must be pectin, acid and sugar present. The finished jelly should be clear in colour with a good set (but not too stiff) and a good fruity flavour. To achieve this only fruits which give a really good set should be used (see jams p 34) unless the good setters are mixed with a lesser setting fruit.

Jellies take longer to make than jams because of the time involved in allowing the cooked pulpy fruit to drip through a jelly bag. However, the smooth results overcome the problems of those who do not like or cannot digest tough skins or pips found in some jams.

The fruit to be used needs little preparation, but thorough washing is essential. Use ripe fruit for preference but slightly underripe is acceptable. Take care with overripe fruit for the pectin content is much lower. Cut out any bad or damaged parts from the fruit and cut up larger varieties roughly— but do not remove peel, cores or pips. Put into a pan with sufficient water to just cover (hard fruits such as currants and quinces need more water and the softer ones less water) and cook slowly until the fruits are really tender so that all the juices can be extracted and all the acid and pectin present are dissolved in the water. The pulp has to be strained through a jelly bag or double thickness of clean tea-towel, sheet or piece of muslin which has previously been scalded. The bag can be tied to a cupboard door, upturned chair, etc, but must be left to drip until no more juice appears—this takes several hours or overnight. Do not prod or squeeze the bag whist straining or the jelly will become cloudy. The strained juice is often called the extract.

The extract is then put into a clean pan with sugar and boiled until setting point is reached, 105°C (221°F) as for jam. On average allow 450g (1lb) sugar to each 500ml (approx 1pt) juice, and heat gently stirring frequently, until the sugar has dissolved, before boiling hard. Setting point is usually reached after about 10 minutes boiling without further stirring. Scum must be removed from the surface before potting with a slotted spoon or by straining through a piece of scalded cloth. Pour into warmed jars, tilted to prevent trapping air bubbles, and cover at once whilst very hot with waxed discs. Dampened cellophane covers can be put on when the jelly is hot or cold. Small jars usually 225–450g ($\frac{1}{2}$–1lb) in size are used for jellies. Take care not to tilt jars until completely cold and set.

It is not practical to quote the yields for jellies because of the varying losses incurred on straining the juice due to the ripeness of the fruit, length of time allowed for dripping, etc.

Note In the jelly recipes, the metric equivalent of 1pt has been rounded down to 500ml, to give the correct consistency.

Apple and Blackberry Jelly

Ingredients

1.8kg (4lb) blackberries
900g (2lb) cooking apples
1.1l (2pt) water
Sugar

Wash the blackberries thoroughly and pick them over and then drain well. Put into a pan. Wash the apples, cut into rough slices removing any bad pieces (but not the cores or skins) and add to the blackberries with the water. Bring to the boil and simmer gently for about an hour or until very tender. Mash the fruit well and then strain through a jelly bag or cloth. Measure the strained juice and return it to a clean pan with 450g (1lb) sugar to each 500ml (approx 1pt) juice. Heat gently until the sugar has dissolved, stirring frequently, then bring up the the boil and boil rapidly until setting point is reached, 105°C (221°F). Remove any scum from the surface and pour into warmed jars. Cover with waxed discs and then a dampened cellophane circle. Cool, label and store in a cool, dark place.

Bramble Jelly

Ingredients

1.8kg (4lb) blackberries
Juice of 2 lemons or 7.5ml (1½ level
    tsp) tartaric or citric acid
450ml (¾pt) water
Sugar

Wash the blackberries thoroughly and pick them over, then drain well. Put into a pan with the lemon juice or acid and the water and bring to the boil. Simmer until really soft and pulpy— about an hour; then mash well. Strain through a jelly bag or cloth, measure the strained juice and return it to a clean pan. Add 450g (1lb) sugar to each 500ml (approx 1pt) strained juice and heat gently until the sugar has dissolved, stirring frequently. Bring to the boil and boil rapidly until setting point is reached, 105°C (221°F). Remove any scum from the surface and pour into warmed jars. Cover with waxed discs and a dampened cellophane circle; then cool, label and store in a cool, dark place.

Jellies

Quince Jelly

Ingredients

1.8kg (4lb) quinces
Thinly pared rind and juice of 3
    lemons or 15g ($\frac{1}{2}$oz) tartaric or
    citric acid
3.4l (6pt) water
Sugar

Wash the quinces well and drain, then cut up into fairly small pieces. Put into a pan with 2.3l (4pt) water and the lemon rind and juice or the acid and bring to the boil. Simmer for about 1 hour or until the fruit is really soft and pulpy. Mash well and then strain through a jelly bag or cloth. Return the quince pulp to the pan with the remaining water and simmer for a further hour to make a second extract, and strain through the bag again. Mix the two strained juices together and measure. Put into a clean pan with

450g (1lb) sugar to each 500ml (approx 1pt) juice and heat gently until the sugar has dissolved. Bring to the boil and boil rapidly until setting point is reached, 105°C (221°F). Remove any scum from the surface and pour into warmed jars. Cover with waxed discs and a dampened cellophane circle then cool, label and store in a cool, dark place.

Note Half quinces and half cooking apples can be used for this recipe especially when quinces are hard to get. It is not then necessary to use the lemon rind and juice or acid, but a little lemon juice does help the flavour.

Crab Apple Jelly

Ingredients

1.8kg (4lb) crab apples
1.4l (2$\frac{1}{2}$pt) water
Few whole cloves, little bruised root
    ginger or thinly pared orange or
    lemon rind (optional)
Sugar

Wash the crab apples and cut into quarters. Put into a preserving pan with the water and add the cloves, ginger, or fruit rind, if used. Bring to the boil and simmer for about 1$\frac{1}{2}$ hours or until the crab apples are very soft and pulpy. Mash the fruit well then strain through a jelly bag or cloth. Measure the strained juice and put into a clean pan with 450g (1lb) sugar to each 500ml (approx 1pt). Heat gently until the sugar has dissolved, stirring frequently, then bring to the boil and boil rapidly until setting point is reached, 105°C (221°F). Remove any scum from the surface then pour into warmed jars. Cover with waxed discs and then a dampened cellophane circle. Cool, label and store in a cool, dark place.

Note Apple jelly is made in the same way as this recipe but as apples give a rather bland jelly, one of the suggested flavourings or a few blackberries, blackcurrants or raspberries should be added to give it more flavour. Also make japonica jelly in this way.

Gooseberry and Elderflower Jelly

Ingredients

1.8kg (4lb) gooseberries
1.4–1.7l (2½–3pt) water
About 16 heads of elderflowers
Sugar

Wash the gooseberries (but don't top and tail) and place in a pan with the water to cover. Wash the elderflowers carefully and add to the pan. Bring to the boil and simmer until the fruit is really soft and pulpy. Strain through a jelly bag or cloth and measure the juice. Put into a clean pan with 450g (1lb) sugar to each 500ml (approx 1pt) juice and heat gently until dissolved. Bring to the boil and boil rapidly until setting point is reached, 105°C

(221 °F). Remove any scum from the surface, pour into warmed jars and cover with waxed discs and then a dampened cellophane circle. Cool, label and store in a cool, dark place.

Note The elderflowers may be omitted. For an orange flavoured gooseberry jelly add the finely pared rinds of 2 oranges in place of the elderflowers.

Gooseberry and Redcurrant Jelly

Ingredients

1.1kg (2½lb) gooseberries
675g (1½lb) redcurrants
Approx 500ml (approx 1pt) water
Sugar

Wash the gooseberries and redcurrants carefully but do not remove stalks or top and tail. Place in a pan with the water (or more if necessary to cover the fruit), and bring to the boil. Simmer until very soft and pulpy, mash well and strain through a jelly bag or cloth. Measure the juice and put into a clean pan. Add 450g (1lb) sugar to each 500ml (approx 1pt) juice and heat gently until dissolved. Bring to the boil and boil rapidly until setting point is reached, 105°C (221°F). Remove any scum from the surface and pour into warmed jars. Cover with waxed discs and then a dampened cellophane circle. Cool, label and store in a cool, dark place.

Note The water can be increased to 900ml–1l (1½–1¾pt) to give a little less concentrated jelly.

Jellies

Apple and Elderberry Jelly

Ingredients

900g (2lb) elderberries
900g (2lb) cooking apples
500ml (approx 1pt) water
Sugar

Wash the elderberries and put into a pan with just sufficient water to cover. Wash the apples and chop up roughly (without removing peel or cores) and put into another pan with just sufficient water to cover. Simmer both fruits gently until very soft and pulpy. Mash the fruits well and strain the combined fruits through a jelly bag or cloth. Measure the juice and put into a clean pan with 450g (1lb) sugar to each 500ml (approx 1pt) juice. Heat gently until the sugar has dissolved, stirring frequently, and then bring to the boil and boil rapidly until setting point is reached, 105°C (221°F). Remove any scum from the surface, pour into warmed jars and cover first with a

waxed disc and then a dampened cellophane circle. Cool, label and store in a cool, dark place.

Blackcurrant and Apple Jelly

Ingredients

675g (1½lb) blackcurrants
675g (1½lb) cooking apples
2.8l (5pt) water
Sugar

Wash the blackcurrants and place in a pan. Wash the apples and cut up roughly (without removing peel or cores) and add to the blackcurrants with the water. Bring to the boil and simmer gently until the contents are very soft and pulpy—about 1 hour. Mash the fruit well and strain through a jelly bag or cloth. Measure the juice into a clean pan and bring to the boil for 5 minutes. Add 450g (1lb) sugar to each 500ml (approx 1pt) juice and heat gently until dissolved. Bring back to the boil and boil rapidly until setting

point is reached, 105°C (221°F).
Remove any scum from the surface and
pour into warmed jars. Cover with
waxed discs and dampened cellophane
circles. Cool, label and store in a cool,
dark place.

Apple and Orange Jelly

Ingredients

4 sweet oranges
1.4kg (3lb) cooking apples
1.7l (3pt) water
Sugar

Wash the oranges and cut into slices
without removing peel or pith. Wash
the apples and roughly chop without
removing the peel or cores. Put both
fruits into a pan with the water and
bring to the boil. Simmer gently until all
the fruit is very tender—$1\frac{1}{4}$–$1\frac{1}{2}$ hours.
Mash well and strain through a jelly
bag or cloth. Measure the strained
juice and put into a clean pan. Add
450g (1lb) sugar to each 500ml
(approx 1 pt) juice and heat gently until
dissolved, stirring frequently. Bring to
the boil and boil rapidly until setting
point is reached, 105°C (221°F).
Remove any scum from the surface and
pour into warmed jars. Cover with
waxed discs and a dampened
cellophane circle. Cool, label and store
in a cool, dark place.

Note A little orange colouring can be
added to the jelly before potting if the
colour is a little pale.

Apple and Lemon Jelly

Make as apple and orange jelly but use
4 lemons in place of the oranges.

Damson Jelly

Ingredients

1.8kg (4lb) damsons
1.1l (2pt) water
Sugar

Wash the damsons well and place in a
pan with the water. Bring to the boil and
simmer gently until the fruit is very soft
—about $\frac{1}{2}$ hour. Mash well and strain
through a jelly bag or cloth. Measure
the juice and put into a clean pan. Add
450g (1lb) sugar to each 500ml
(approx 1pt) strained juice and heat
gently until the sugar has dissolved,
stirring frequently. Bring to the boil and
boil rapidly until setting point is
reached, 105°C (221°F). Remove any
scum from the surface, pour into
warmed jars and cover first with waxed
discs and then with dampened
cellophane circles. Cool, label and
store in a cool, dark place.

Note Damson jelly is often made in
preference to jam because of the
difficulty of removing all the stones
from the jam. For damson and apple
jelly use 900g (2lb) damsons, 1.8kg
(4lb) cooking apples and 1.4l ($2\frac{1}{2}$pt)
water; cook the damsons and roughly
chopped apples, without removing
peel or cores, together and continue
as above.

Jellies

Redcurrant Jelly

This is a popular jelly for serving with meats and for this purpose it should have a firm consistency and piquant flavour.

Ingredients

1.4kg (3lb) redcurrants
500ml (approx 1pt) water
Sugar

Wash the fruit without removing the stalks and place in a saucepan with the water. Bring to the boil and simmer gently until very soft and pulpy. Mash well and strain through a jelly bag or cloth. Measure the strained juice and put into a clean pan adding 450g (1lb) sugar to each 500ml (approx 1pt) juice. Heat gently until dissolved, stirring frequently, and bring to the boil. Boil rapidly until setting point is reached, 105°C (221°F), then remove any scum from the surface. Pour into warmed jars quickly. This must be done quickly for a concentrated redcurrant jelly tends to set fast. Cover with waxed discs and then dampened cellophane circles. Cool, label and store in a cool, dark place.

Note For a less concentrated and slightly less firm jelly, increase the water to 900ml–1l (1½–1¾pt).

Redcurrant and Apple Jelly

A more economical jelly than redcurrant jelly, still suitable to serve with meats but also good as a preserve.

Ingredients

900g (2lb) redcurrants
900g (2lb) cooking apples
1.4l (2½pt) water
Sugar

Wash the redcurrants without removing the stalks and put into a saucepan. Wash the apples and roughly chop or slice without removing the peel or cores, and add to the pan with the water. Bring to the boil and simmer until the fruits are really tender and mushy. Mash well and strain through a jelly bag or cloth. Measure the strained juice into a clean pan and add 450g (1lb) sugar to each 500ml (approx 1pt) juice. Heat gently until dissolved, stirring frequently and then bring to the boil. Boil rapidly until setting point is reached, 105°C (221°F) then remove any scum from the surface. Pour into warmed jars, cover with waxed discs, then dampened cellophane circles and cool, label and store in a cool, dark place.

Mint Jelly (1)

This is a pleasant mint-flavoured apple jelly suitable for use as a preserve or to serve as a mild accompaniment to meats.

Ingredients

1.4kg (3lb) green skinned cooking
    apples
1.3l (2¼pt) water, approx
A bunch of freshly picked mint
Juice of 2 lemons or 5ml (1 level tsp)
    tartaric or citric acid
Sugar
Green colouring (optional)
45–60ml (3–4tbsp) freshly chopped
    mint or a few sprigs of mint, bruised

distributed through the set jelly. Pour into small warmed jars, cover with waxed discs and then dampened cellophane circles. Cool, label and store in a cool, dark place.

Mint Jelly (2)

With added vinegar this jelly has a piquant flavour suitable to serve with meats.

Ingredients

1.4kg (3lb) green skinned cooking
    apples
500ml (approx 1pt) water
A bunch of freshly picked mint
750ml (1¼pt) white distilled vinegar
Sugar
45–60ml (3–4tbsp) freshly chopped
    mint
Green colouring (optional)

Wash the apples and chop roughly without removing the peel or cores. Put into a pan with the water and bunch of mint and bring to the boil. Simmer gently until the fruit is really soft and pulpy, stirring occasionally to prevent it sticking. Add the vinegar and simmer for a further 5 minutes. Strain through a jelly bag or cloth and measure the strained juice into a clean pan. Add 450g (1lb) sugar to each 500ml (approx 1pt) juice and heat gently until dissolved, stirring frequently. Bring to the boil and boil rapidly until setting point is reached. Remove any scum from the surface, stir in the mint and a few drops of green colouring, if liked. Leave to stand for a few minutes before pouring into small warm jars. Cover with waxed discs and a dampened cellophane circle. Cool, label and store in a cool, dark place.

The greener the skins of the apples the better, for red skinned ones do not give a good coloured jelly. Wash the apples, chop roughly (without removing peel or cores), and put into a pan with the water, mint and lemon juice or acid. Bring to the boil and simmer until soft and pulpy. Mash well and strain through a jelly bag or cloth. Measure the strained juice and put into a clean pan with 450g (1lb) sugar to each 500ml (approx 1pt) juice. Heat gently until the sugar has dissolved, stirring frequently, then bring to the boil and boil for 5 minutes. Either add the chopped mint (or add the bruised mint to the jelly for 3–4 minutes whilst continuing to boil). Remove the sprigs of mint and continue to boil until setting point is reached, 105°C (221°F). Remove any scum from the surface and stir in a little green colouring, if liked. Leave to stand until a thin skin forms on the surface, if using chopped mint, as this helps to keep it evenly

Marmalades

A marmalade is a jam, jelly or pulp in which slices or pieces of peel or fruit are suspended. Seville oranges, lemons, grapefruit and limes are the most usual 'marmalade fruits' but sweet oranges and tangerines can also be combined with these fruits to give other flavours.

The method of making marmalade is basically very similar to jam making but extra time is needed to prepare and cook the tough peel of the citrus fruit which would otherwise spoil the finished marmalade. The pectin required to set the finished marmalade is found in the pips and the white pith so the pips must be tied in a muslin bag and the peel with pith attached (although if very thick, some may be pared off), finely shredded.

The peel can be evenly shredded by hand, or by using a slicer to do the job—however hand shredding is always preferred. The peel can also be minced but this gives a thick jam-like finished preserve, which some people do not like. The shredded peel (fine or medium according to taste) can be soaked in the measured water overnight before cooking to help soften the peel but it is not essential. The cooking time is longer than for jams—usually at least an hour—and because of this more water is used to allow for the evaporation. The contents of the pan should be reduced by about half, and the peel really soft before adding the sugar—failure to do so is one of the most common reasons for marmalade failing to set and gives tough and chewy pieces in the finished preserve. This first softening process can be done in a pressure cooker to save time allowing 600ml (1pt) water to each 450g (1lb) fruit, but the amount cooked at one time is much smaller. 900g (2lb) is the usual amount to make in a pressure cooker but follow the manufacturer's instructions. Once tender add the sugar and proceed as usual.

Once the sugar has been added and slowly dissolved as for jams, the rapid boiling to reach setting point usually takes a little longer than with jams and the longer the boiling, the darker the colour of the finished marmalade. A little black treacle can be added with the sugar if you like really dark marmalade, ie 25g (1oz) to each 2.7kg (6lb) sugar. Allow the marmalade to stand in the pan for 5–10 minutes after removing the scum from the surface before potting to prevent the peel rising in the jar. Place the waxed discs immediately on the hot marmalade. The cellophane covers can be put on hot or cold as preferred but are more usually added when the marmalade is cold. Label and store in a cool, dark place. Allowing the marmadade to mature for a few weeks before use is advisable but it can be used at once. Marmadades should keep well for at least two years if properly made, covered and stored.

When making jelly marmalade it is essential to test for pectin content before adding the sugar, or the finished marmalade may not set. To do this take 5ml (1tsp) of the juice from the cooked fruit (ie just before adding the sugar) and put into a glass. When cool add 15ml (1tbsp) methylated spirits and shake well. Leave for 1 minute and if it forms a good jelly clot there is plenty of pectin. If it does not form a clot then it requires extra pectin which can be obtained either by boiling further to reduce the bulk and then retesting before adding the sugar or by adding lemon juice, 30ml (2tbsp) to each 1.8kg (4lb) fruit and then retesting. This test can also be used for jams, and jellies which use fruit with low pectin content to be certain of a good set.

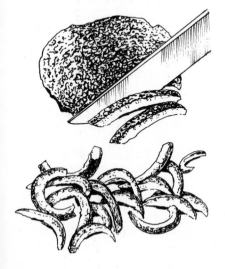

Note Marmalade fruits with a short season like Seville oranges and limes can be scrubbed, packed in suitable containers and frozen until required. The semi-thawed fruit should then be cooked by the method for lemon marmalade (see p 54).

Seville Orange Marmalade

Ingredients

1.4kg (3lb) Seville oranges
2.6–3.4l (4½–6pt) water
Juice of 2 lemons
2.7kg (6lb) sugar

Wash the fruit thoroughly, scrubbing off any stubborn marks. Cut the fruit in halves, squeeze out the juice and pips and remove the membrane. Tie the pips and membrane in a muslin bag. Cut the peel into thin shreds (or to taste) and put into a preserving pan with the orange juice, water, lemon juice and bag of pips. Bring to the boil and simmer gently, uncovered, until the contents of the pan are reduced by about half and the peel is really tender —about 2 hours. Remove the muslin bag and squeeze out all the juice from it. Add the sugar and stir until completely dissolved. Bring to the boil and boil rapidly until setting point is reached, 105°C (221°F). Remove any scum from the surface and leave to stand for about 5–10 minutes. Pour into warmed jars and cover with waxed discs (wax side downwards) whilst hot. Finish with cellophane tops when hot or cold and then label and store in a cool, dark place. Approx yield : 4.5kg (10lb).

Marmalades

Mixed Fruit Marmalade

Ingredients

4 lemons
2 sweet oranges } total weight
2 grapefruit } 1.4kg (3lb)
2.6–3.4l (4½–6pt) water
2.7kg (6lb) sugar

Wash the fruit thoroughly. Cut lemons and oranges in halves and squeeze out the juice and pips. Pare off the rind of the grapefruit without too much of the white pith, then peel off the remainder of the pith and any stringy parts of the fruit and put into a muslin bag with the lemon and orange pips. Either finely shred, coarsely shred or mince all the peels according to taste and put into a preserving pan with the fruit juices. Roughly chop up the grapefruit flesh discarding the pips and add to the pan with the water. Add the muslin bag and bring to the boil. Simmer for 1–1½ hours or until the peel is really soft and the contents of the pan reduced by about half. Remove the muslin bag, squeezing out all the juice and stir in the sugar until dissolved. Bring to the boil and boil rapidly until setting point is reached, 105°C (221°F). Remove any scum from the surface and leave to stand for about 10 minutes. Pour into warmed jars and cover with waxed discs at once. Finish with cellophane tops when hot or cold. Label and store in a cool, dark place. Approx yield : 4.5kg (10lb).

Note This marmalade can be made at any time of the year for it does not require Seville oranges.

Lemon or Lime Marmalade

Ingredients

1.4kg (3lb) thin skinned lemons or limes
2.6–3.4l (4½–6pt) water
2.7kg (6lb) sugar

This marmalade can be made in the same way as Seville orange marmalade, or in the following way :
Weigh the preserving pan before you start. Wash whichever fruit you use and remove the stem end. Put the fruit with the water in a pan with a tight fitting lid and simmer gently for 1½–2 hours or until the fruit is really soft. Remove from the pan and slice or chop the fruit finely, separating out the pips. (A knife and fork is the best thing to use for this.) Return the fruit and juice to the cooking liquor and weigh. It should weigh 2.3kg (5lb) (plus weight of pan) but if not, boil it further until it does. Add the sugar and stir until dissolved then boil rapidly until setting point is reached. Remove any scum from the surface and leave to stand for 5–10 minutes. Pour into warmed jars and cover immediately with waxed discs. Finish with cellophane tops when hot or cold. Label and store in a cool, dark place. Approx yield : 4.5kg (10lb).

Note It is not necessary to weigh the pan if you test the cooked fruit for pectin content (see p 34) before adding the sugar. This method can also be used for other fruit marmalades and is especially good for using frozen whole fruit.

Orange Jelly Marmalade

Ingredients

900g (2lb) Seville oranges
2.6l (4½pt) water
Juice of 2 large lemons
1.4kg (3lb) sugar

To make sure of a good set this marmalade must be tested for pectin content (see p 34) before adding the sugar.

Scrub the oranges and dry and then pare off the rind free of any of the white pith. Shred this peel very finely and put into a pan with 600ml (1pt) water. Bring to the boil, cover and simmer for about 1½ hours or until very tender. Meanwhile roughly chop up the remaining fruit including pith etc and put into a pan with 1.4l (2½pt) water and the lemon juice. Bring to the boil and simmer in a covered pan for about 2 hours until really soft and pulpy. Strain the orange shreds and add the liquid to the cooked pulp. Strain this pulp through a jelly bag for about 15 minutes into a bowl, without squeezing it. Return the pulp to the pan with the remaining water and simmer for a further 20 minutes. Strain the pulp again until it stops dripping and then mix it with the first extract. Test the extract for pectin and if it doesn't clot, boil it rapidly to reduce a little and retest. Add the sugar, stirring until dissolved, then add the orange shreds. Boil rapidly until setting point is reached, 105°C (221°F). Remove any scum from the surface and leave to stand for 15 minutes before pouring into warmed jars. Cover at once with waxed discs and finish with cellophane tops when hot or cold. Do not move or tilt the jars until set. Label and store in a cool, dark place. Approx yield : 2.3kg (5lb).

Ginger Marmalade

Ingredients

3 Seville oranges
1.4l (2½pt) water
675g (1½lb) cooking apples
1.5kg (3¼lb) sugar
100g (4oz) preserved ginger, finely chopped
10ml (2 level tsp) ground ginger

Wash the oranges thoroughly then remove the peel. Shred this peel finely and put into a pan. Chop up the flesh separating the tough membranes and pips and tie these in a muslin bag. Add the flesh, juice and muslin bag to the pan with the water and bring to the boil. Simmer for about 1½ hours or until the contents of the pan are reduced by half and the peel is very soft. Remove the muslin bag squeezing out all the juice. Meanwhile peel, core and chop the apples roughly and put into a pan with 45–60ml (3–4tbsp) water. Simmer gently until well pulped then stir into the cooked and reduced orange mixture with the sugar, chopped and ground ginger. When the sugar has dissolved, boil rapidly until setting point is reached, 105°C (221°F). Remove any scum from the surface and leave to stand for 15 minutes before pouring into warmed jars. Cover with waxed discs immediately and with cellophane covers when hot or cold. Label and store in a cool, dark place. Approx yield : 2.3kg (5lb).

Bottling

The success or failure of home bottling depends largely on efficient sterilization. The object of preserving fruits in bottles is to kill the yeasts and moulds already present in the cells on the surface of the fruits and to prevent them and others spreading into the container which would cause fermentation and eventually rotting in the jars. This is done by heating the fruit to sterilize and inactivate the enzymes present and then sealing whilst hot.

Bottling Jars and Covers

These are wide-necked glass jars with either glass caps or metal discs which are secured by screw bands or clips. A new rubber ring or metal disc fitted with a special seal should be used each time for bottling, but the jars can be used many times provided they are clean and sound. Jars are widely available in sizes ranging from 450g (1lb) up to 1.8kg (4lb), as are the replacement tops. A check of the soundness of bottles must be made before starting. To do this, fill the jar with water, put on the lid, then turn jar upside down and leave for 10 minutes. If there is a leak, it will then be apparent. Wash all jars thoroughly in hot soapy water, rinse out but do not dry for the fruit slips more easily into a wet jar.

What Can I Bottle?

Almost any type of fruit can be bottled provided you follow the general rules for preparing and processing. The fruit used must be fresh and sound, clean (wash if dirty or gritty) and just ripe.

Do not use overripe fruit for it tends to ferment more easily. Also grade fruits into sizes for each bottle and use a bottle of the appropriate size.

Preparation of Fruits for Bottling

Apples

(slices) Peel, core and slice or cut into rings. During preparation prevent discolouration by immersing in a brine solution (10ml/2 level tsp salt to 1.1l/2pt cold water). Rinse quickly in cold water before packing into jars.

Apples

(solid pack) Prepare as above for slices then blanch in boiling water for $1\frac{1}{2}$–3 minutes until the fruit is pliable and just tender. Drain and pack tightly into jars.

Apricots

(whole) Remove stalks and rinse in cold water. Or cut fruit in half carefully by twisting in half and removing the stone. Pack quickly before cut surfaces begin to discolour. Some stones can be cracked and the kernels added to the jar.

Blackberries

Discard any unsound fruit, stalks and leaves, and wash.

Blackberries with Apples

Prepare the apples as for solid pack then mix with the washed blackberries and pack into jars.

Blackcurrants and Redcurrants

Pick over carefully, remove stalks and wash.

Cherries

(whole) Remove stalks and wash fruit. (stoned) Remove stones with a cherry stoner or small knife collecting any juice to add to the fruit. To improve the colour and flavour of black or white cherries add 5ml (1 level tsp) citric acid to each 2.3l (4pt) syrup.

Damsons

Remove stalks and wash.

Figs

Remove stems, peel if liked. Add 2.5ml ($\frac{1}{2}$ level tsp) citric acid to each 600ml (1pt) syrup used to help the figs keep well. Pack with an equal weight of syrup.

Gooseberries

Use small green fruit for pies and the larger ones for stewed fruit. Top and tail, taking a small slice from each end of the fruit or prick the skins well to prevent shrivelling when preserved in syrup.

Peaches

Dip in boiling water for $\frac{1}{2}$ minute then plunge into cold water; peel off the skins. Leave whole or cut in halves and remove the stones as for apricots.

Pears

(cooking) Not the best fruit for bottling as they are very hard, but they can be prepared as for dessert pears and then stewed gently in syrup— 100–175g (4–6oz) sugar to 600ml (1pt) water—until tender. Pack into jars.

Pears

(dessert) Peel, halve and core carefully using a teaspoon. During preparation put into a brine solution using 10ml (2 level tsp) salt and 7.5ml ($1\frac{1}{2}$ level tsp) citric acid to each 1.1l (2pt) water. Rinse in cold water before packing.

Plums and Gages

(whole) Remove stalks and wash. (halved) Only possible with free-stone varieties. Make a cut round the fruit, twist in half and remove stone. Crack some stones and add the kernels to the jars. Pack quickly to prevent discolouration.

Quinces

Prepare as for cooking pears and preserve in small jars for they are usually only used in small quantities and mixed with other fruit.

Raspberries and Loganberries

Hull, pick over carefully and do not wash unless absolutely essential.

Rhubarb

Use thick stalks for made up dishes and the tender young stalks to serve as stewed fruit. Cut into 2.5–5cm (1–2in) lengths and pack carefully into jars. It is easier to pack if soaked overnight in hot syrup to soften the fruit. Use the syrup for topping up.

Strawberries

These do not really bottle well but can be done by soaking overnight in the syrup. Then pack drained fruit into jars. Boil syrup until reduced to its original amount before adding to the jars.

Tomatoes

See p 62 for method and bottling instructions.

Bottling

Packing the Fruit

Pack into jars (with inside of jar wet) in layers using a long-handled packing spoon or the handle of a wooden spoon. It must be packed tightly but without bruising or damaging the fruit. Some large fruits need to be halved, sliced or cut into rings. The tighter packed and fuller the jar, the less risk there is of the fruit rising after the sterilizing process, which can cause some shrinkage.

Syrup

Fruit may be preserved in syrup or water, but syrup usually gives a better flavour and colour to the fruit and keeps it better after long storage, but it does cause the fruit to rise in the jars. The strength of syrup used can vary but 225g (8oz) sugar to 600ml (1pt) water is the usual strength although for tightly packed fruits the syrup should be heavier, ie 275–300g (10–11oz) per 600ml (1pt). Use granulated or loaf sugar and dissolve it in half the water, then bring to the boil for 1 minute, remove from the heat, add the remaining water and leave to cool. This saves time in cooling syrup for use with the slow water bath method of sterilizing using a thermometer (see p 58). Use hot (not boiling) syrup for the quick water bath method and boiling syrup for oven methods and pressure cookers.

When to add the syrup depends on which method of sterilizing is used, so see separate methods, but when jars are full, in all methods give the bottles a quick jerk to free as many air bubbles as possible before sealing down.

Sterilizing

There are several ways of sterilizing the bottles but the two most often used are the water bath method and the oven method (see pp 58 and 60). A pressure cooker can also be used (see p 62).

Checking for Seal

After processing the bottles, it is important to test for an airtight seal. To do this remove the screw band or clip and try to lift the jar by the cap or disc. If it holds firm then there is a good seal but if it comes off there may be a flaw in the rim of the jar or cover. If several fail to seal it is more likely to be a fault in the sterilizing process. The fruit can be reprocessed but it will lose a lot of its quality so is probably best used up quickly.

The Water Bath Method (Slow) of Sterilizing

This method of sterilizing is the more accurate way but it does require a large pan (ie an old zinc bath or bucket or a very large saucepan) which is about 5cm (2in) deeper than the tops of the bottles, a thermometer (a sugar one will do), bottling tongs (or wooden washing tongs) to remove the bottles quickly from the water bath, and a false bottom for the water bath which can be a metal grid, wooden trellis, wad of newspapers or folded cloths.

1 Fill up the fruit filled jars with cold syrup and put the metal discs and screw bands in place (or the rubber bands and glass discs) and then turn the screw bands back a quarter turn.
2 Put the jars in the water bath on the hob and cover completely with cold water (or at least up to the necks if

complete submersion is impossible).
3 Heat the water gently until it reaches 54 °C (130 °F) in one hour, checking the temperature regularly with the thermometer then continue heating to reach the processing temperature as suggested on the chart, taking about half an hour and checking the temperature regularly.
4 Maintain this temperature for the time stated on the chart.
5 Remove the jars carefully with the tongs and stand on a wooden surface or a thick pad of newspapers.
6 Tighten the screw bands immediately.

The quick water bath method can be used if you do not have a thermometer. Fill the packed jars with hot (but not boiling) syrup. Cover as for the slow water bath method and put into a bath of warm water. Bring the water to simmering point in 25–30 minutes and keep at simmering point for the time stated on the chart.

Note Soft and stone fruits can be bottled as a pulp to make pies, sauces, ice cream, etc. Stew in the minimum of water until only just cooked. At this stage the fruit can be liquidized and/or sieved if liked. Pour the boiling pulp into hot jars and put on the covers as above. Immerse in a pan of hot water up to the necks and bring the water up to boiling point. Keep boiling for 5 minutes, then remove the jars and screw down immediately. Cool, label and store.

Sterilization Times for the Water Bath Method (as suggested by the Long Ashton Research Station)

Type of Fruit	Slow Method	Quick Method
Soft fruit (normal pack) : blackberries, currants, loganberries, mulberries, raspberries, gooseberries and rhubarb for made-up dishes, apples (sliced)	Raise from cold in 90 minutes and maintain as below 74 °C (165 °F) for 10 minutes	Raise from warm 38 °C (100 °F), to simmering 88 °C (190 °F) in 25–30 minutes and maintain as below For 2 minutes
Soft fruit (tight pack) : as above, including gooseberries and rhubarb to serve as stewed fruit Stone fruit (whole) : Apricots, cherries, damsons, gages and plums	82 °C (180 °F) for 15 minutes	For 10 minutes
Apples (solid pack), apricots (halved), nectarines, peaches pineapple, plums (halved)	82 °C (180 °F) for 15 minutes	For 20 minutes
Figs, pears	88 °C (190 °F) for 30 minutes	For 40 minutes

Bottling

The Oven Method of Sterilizing

The advantage of the oven method of sterilizing is that jars can be processed one at a time and no special equipment is required. It isn't quite so exact as the water bath method because the temperature throughout the oven doesn't stay constant all the time and it is easier to overcook the fruit. Use only one central shelf in the oven and stand the bottles far enough apart to allow the heat to circulate freely. Tall jars are not suitable for this method. There is a wet pack and dry pack method for sterilizing in the oven.

Wet Pack

This method avoids the difficulty of filling hot jars with boiling syrup. Heat the oven to 150 °C (300 °F) mark 2. Pack the warmed jars with fruit then fill with boiling syrup or water to within 2.5cm (1in) of the top. Put on the rubber rings and glass caps or metal discs but not the clips or screw bands. Stand the filled jars on a baking sheet padded with newspaper (to catch any liquid that boils over) leaving 5cm (2in) between each jar. Place in the centre of the oven and process for the time stated on the chart below. Remove the jars one by one to a wooden surface or wad of newspaper and put on clips or screw bands—screwing the bands as tightly as possible. Leave until quite cold then test for airtightness. Label and store.

Dry Pack

Heat the oven to 130 °C (250 °F) mark $\frac{1}{2}$. Pack the prepared fruit into bottles but do not add any liquid. Put on the caps but *not* the rubber rings, metal discs with rims, screw bands or clips. Stand the jars on a newspaper lined baking sheet with 5cm (2in) between each one. Put into the centre of the oven and process for the time stated on the chart. Remove the jars one at a time from the oven to a wooden surface and fill up each bottle with fruit from an extra bottle if the contents have shrunk at all. Fill up immediately with boiling syrup and give each bottle a good jerk to dispel the air bubbles ; then cover with the rubber bands, caps or metal discs and secure with clips or put on the screw bands tightly. Leave to get cold and test for air-tightness. The success of this method depends on filling the jars and sealing them as quickly as possible after being taken from the oven. (This dry pack method is not recommended for fruits which discolour in the air, eg apples, pears and peaches.)

Note With both oven methods, the time required varies with the different types of fruit, tightness of the pack in the bottle and the total load in the oven at one time. The load is calculated according to the total capacity of the jars.

Processing Times for Oven Methods (as recommended by the Long Ashton Research Station)

Type of Fruit	Wet Pack		Dry Pack	
	Pre-heat oven to 150°C (300° F) mark 2. Process time varies with quantity in oven, as shown below		Pre-heat oven to 130°C (250°F) mark ½. Process time varies with quantity in oven, as shown below	
	Quantity	Time in minutes	Quantity	Time in minutes
Soft fruit (normal Pack): blackberries, currants, loganberries, raspberries, gooseberries and rhubarb (for made-up dishes)	450g–1.8kg (1–4lb) 2–4.5kg (4½–10lb)	30–40 45–60	450g–1.8kg (1–4lb) 2–4.5kg (4½–10lb)	45–55 60–75
Apples (sliced)	450g–1.8kg (1–4lb) 2–4.5kg (4½–10lb)	30–40 45–60	Not recommended	
Soft fruit (tight packs): as above including gooseberries and rhubarb for stewed fruit	450g–1.8kg (1–4lb) 2–4.5kg (4½–10lb)	40–50 55–70	450g–1.8kg (1–4lb) 2–4.5kg (4½–10lb)	55–70 75–90
Stone fruit (dark whole): cherries, plums, damsons	As soft fruit (tight pack)		As soft fruit (tight pack)	
Stone fruit (light whole): apricots, cherries, gages, plums	As above		Not recommended	
Apples (solid pack), apricots (halved), nectarines, peaches, plums (halved), strawberries (soaked)	450g–1.8kg (1–4lb) 2–4.5kg (4½–10lb)	50–60 65–80	Not recommended	
Figs	450g–1.8kg (1–4lb) 2–4.5kg (4½–10lb)	60–70 75–90	450g–1.8kg (1–4lb) 2–4.5kg (4½–10lb)	80–100 105–125
Pears	As figs		Not recommended	

Bottling

Bottling Tomatoes

There are three different methods of bottling tomatoes :

Whole unpeeled tomatoes (recommended for oven sterilizing). Use small and medium ripe but firm fruit, uniform in size. Remove stalks, wash or wipe and pack into jars. Fill up with a brine of 10ml (2 level tsp) salt to each 1.1l (2pt) water.

Solid pack (no water added). Use any sized firm fruit and peel after dipping first into boiling water for $\frac{1}{2}$ minute then into cold water. Leave small fruit whole, but halve or quarter larger fruit. Pack really tightly with no air spaces making it impossible to add water. To improve the flavour sprinkle about 5ml (1 level tsp) salt and 2.5ml ($\frac{1}{2}$ level tsp) sugar over the fruit to fill a 450g (1lb) jar.

In their own juice. Peel tomatoes as for solid pack and pack tightly into jars. Stew a few tomatoes in a covered pan with 5ml (1 level tsp) salt to each 900g (2lb) fruit, strain the juice and use to fill up the jars.

With pressure cooker sterilizing for whole or halved tomatoes in brine, process the tomatoes for 5 minutes at low (2.25kg/5lb) pressure following pressure cooker method on p 63.

Pressure Cooker Method

This is a much shorter form of processing with an exact temperature control. The cooker must have a 'low'

Processing Chart for Tomatoes

	Oven Method		Water Bath Method	
	Wet Pack Pre-heat oven to 150°C (300°F) mark 2, process as below	Dry Pack Pre-heat oven to 130°C (250°F) mark $\frac{1}{2}$, process as below	Slow Method Raise from cold in 90 minutes and maintain as below	Quick Method Raise from warm 38°C (100°F) to simmering 88°C (190°F) in 25–30 minutes and maintain for :
Whole tomatoes	450g–1.8kg (1–4lb) for 60–70 minutes 2–4.5kg ($4\frac{1}{2}$–10lb) for 75–90 minutes	450g–1.8kg (1–4lb) for 80–100 minutes 2–4.5kg ($4\frac{1}{2}$–10lb) for 105–125 minutes	88°C (190°F) for 30 minutes	40 minutes
Solid pack tomatoes (halved or quartered)	450g–1.8kg (1–4lb) for 70–80 minutes 2–4.5kg ($4\frac{1}{2}$–10lb) for 85–100 minutes	Not recommended for solid packs	88°C (190°F) for 40 minutes	50 minutes

2.25kg (5lb) pressure control and unless it has a domed lid, only the 450g (1lb) jars will fit in.

Prepare the fruit as for ordinary bottling taking note of the additional information on the chart below. Pack the fruit into clean warm jars up to the top and cover with boiling syrup or water to within 2.5cm (1in) of the top of the bottles. Position the rubber bands and caps or metal discs and add clips or put on screw bands tightly and then give a quarter turn back. Heat the jars gently by standing in a bowl or pan of boiling water. Put the rack in the bottom of the pressure cooker and add 900ml (1½pt) water (with 15ml [1tbsp] vinegar to prevent discolouration). Bring to the boil, pack the bottles into the cooker with newspaper between each to prevent them touching and put on the lid without the weight. Heat until steam comes from the vent then put on the low (2.25kg/5lb) pressure control and bring to pressure on a low heat. Reduce the heat and maintain for the time given in the chart. It is important to keep the pressure constant for any change will cause liquid to be lost from the jars and this may cause under processing. Remove the pressure cooker from the heat and leave to cool and reduce the pressure for 10 minutes at room temperature, before removing the lid. (This time completes the processing.)

Take out the jars and tighten screw bands. Leave to cool, label and store.

Pressure Cooker Method

Type of Fruit	Processing time in minutes at 'low' 2.25kg (5lb) pressure
Apples (quartered) ; apricots and plums (whole), blackberries, loganberries, raspberries, cherries, currants, damsons, gooseberries, rhubarb (in 5cm (2in) lengths)	1 minute
Plums and apricots (halved and stoned)	3 minutes
Pears (eating and cooking) : hard cooking pears can be pressure cooked for 3–5 minutes before packing in jars	5 minutes
Strawberries	Not recommended
Soft fruit (solid pack) : Put the fruit in a large bowl, cover with boiling syrup, (175g (6oz) sugar to 600ml (1pt) water) and leave overnight. Drain, pack and cover with same syrup. Process as usual	3 minutes
Pulped fruit (eg apples) : Prepare as for stewing. Pressure cook with 150ml (¼pt) water at high, 6.75kg (15lb) pressure for 2–3 minutes, then sieve. Fill jars whilst hot and process	1 minute

Further reading from David & Charles

GOOD FOOD GROWING GUIDE
Gardening and Living Nature's Way
John Bond and the Staff of 'Mother Earth'
A new-look growing guide to healthier and happier living
241 × 148mm illustrated

ECONOMY COOK BOOK
Mary Griffiths
A guide to how to cope with rising food and housekeeping prices and still produce tasty and nutritious meals
216 × 138mm

COST-EFFECTIVE SELF-SUFFICIENCY
or The Middle-Class Peasant
Eve and Terence McLaughlin
A practical guide to self-sufficiency, proving that life as 'middle-class peasants' is not only viable but enormously enjoyable and satisfying
247 × 171mm illustrated

EAT CHEAPLY AND WELL
Brenda Sanctuary
Rising food prices make this up-to-the-minute book a must for today's housewives
216 × 138mm illustrated

GROWPLAN VEGETABLE BOOK
A Month-by-Month Guide
Peter Peskett and Geoff Amos
A practical, easy-reference guide to growing super vegetables, and fruit too, month by month
250 × 200mm illustrated

GROWING FOOD UNDER GLASS:
1001 Questions Answered
Adrienne and Peter Oldale
An indispensable guide to setting up and maintaining every kind of glasshouse, together with an A–Z rundown of the familiar and unusual fruit and vegetables to be grown
210 × 148mm illustrated

GROWING FRUIT:
1001 Questions Answered
Adrienne and Peter Oldale
Answers all the questions a novice might ask about pests and diseases, choice of tree shapes and varieties, and pruning techniques
210 × 148mm illustrated

GROWING VEGETABLES:
1001 Questioned Answered
Adrienne and Peter Oldale
All you need to know about growing vegetables in a simple question and answer format
210 × 148mm illustrated

COMPLETE BOOK OF HERBS AND SPICES
Claire Loewenfeld and Philippa Back
A comprehensive guide to every aspect of herbs and spices—their history and traditions. cultivation, uses in the kitchen, and health and cosmetics
242 × 184mm illustrated

British Library Cataloguing in Publication Data

Wadey, Rosemary
    Preserving and pickling.—(Penny pinchers).
    1. Fruit—Preservation—Amateurs' manuals
    2. Jam—Amateurs' manuals 3. Chutney—
    Amateurs' manuals 4. Pickles—Amateurs'
    manuals
    I. Title II. Series
    641.8'52   TX612,F7

ISBN 0–7153–7551–2

© David & Charles Ltd 1978

Set in Univers
and printed in Great Britain
by Redwood Burn Limited
for David & Charles (Publishers) Limited
Brunel House Newton Abbot Devon

Published in the United States of America
by David & Charles Inc
North Pomfret Vermont 05053 USA

Published in Canada
by Douglas David & Charles Limited
1875 Welch Street North Vancouver BC